Behind the Scenes at
Time Team

Tim Taylor

Photographs by

Chris Bennett

CHANNEL 4 BOOKS

Dedicated to Katie T. and Les and Joan Taylor.

First published in 1998 by Channel 4 Books, an imprint of Macmillan Publishers Ltd,
25 Eccleston Place, London SW1W 9NF and Basingstoke.

Associated companies throughout the world.

ISBN 0 7522 1327 X

Text © Tim Taylor, 1998
Photographs © Chris Bennett, 1998

10 9 8 7 6

A CIP catalogue record for this book is available from the British Library.

Design by DW Design
Line illustrations by Victor Ambrus

All photographs were shot with Nikon F4S and F90X cameras, fitted with Nikkor lenses
ranging from 16mm to 300mm, and on Kodak Elitechrome film stock.
Processed in London by Sky Photographic.

Colour reproduction by Aylesbury Studios Limited
Printed in Italy by New Interlitho S.P.A.

The section on scheduling on page 22 is taken from the leaflet *Scheduling Monuments*
produced by English Heritage in 1997.

This book accompanies the television series *Time Team* made by Videotext Communications
in association with Picture House Television Company for Channel 4.
Series Producer: Tim Taylor
Executive Producer: Philip Clarke

Behind the Scenes at
Time Team

Contents

Introduction

Time Team, Channel 4's award-winning series on archaeology has completed over forty programmes. Each one was a struggle to unlock the secrets of the past in just three days; and each one contributed unique information to the historical record.

During the six years that I and other members of the *Time Team* have been working on the series, we have repeatedly been asked about what goes on behind the scenes. Does it really take three days? Is Tony Robinson interested in archaeology? What was our most exciting find? How do we choose the sites?

This book answers these questions and others, and provides an insight into what happens behind the scenes of Britain's most popular archaeological programme. The photographer, Chris Bennett, was given unique access to all the stages of the production process from the initial choice of sites, through research and filming to the final stages of post-production. Chris, who has worked on many 'behind the scenes' books on subjects ranging from the Red Arrows to the famous Harrods store in Knightsbridge, describes this access as 'exceptional'. It meant he was able to get the kind of candid shots that reflect the tensions and drama that inevitably result when a team of more than fifty people battles for three days with the often intractable secrets of the past.

Each of the sites selected for *Behind the Scenes at Time Team* created its own particular challenges, both in terms of the research and background material needed to bring a specific historical period to light, and in the archaeological techniques used to locate the evidence.

Historically the book ranges from prehistory to the more recent past. A Palaeolithic cave, Josiah Wedgwood's first pottery factory, ironworks for the Roman fleet, a lost dockyard used by Henry V's navy and a bomber that crashed in the Second World War provide the main stories.

The environmental and working conditions for each site presented different challenges. We struggled in the depths of an underground tunnel and searched a vast area of landscape in the rolling Sussex countryside. We were up to our ears in tarmac, concrete and bricks in the middle of a town, and coped with unexploded munitions on an environmentally sensitive site in the Norfolk marshes.

Each site required different archaeological techniques and these are described in detail, along with the thinking behind the strategies we followed. In any creative process there are tensions between opposing elements. These are necessary and on *Time Team* we have to find a balance between the realities of an archaeological dig and making a film with a strong story line.

Tension can surface most obviously as we move towards the end of a shoot, when we are often faced with a decision as to whether or not more trenches should be opened on the third day. The last few trenches have often held the key to a site and I have to try to get more work done on the final day if I believe this might answer the critical question that the programme and archaeology are asking. However, I also have to respect the archaeologists' need to ensure that whatever we do can be properly recorded and excavated in the time we have left. From the start I have had an unwritten agreement with Mick Aston that I will not push the archaeology beyond the point where he feels comfortable. On the other hand, both he and Phil Harding realize that I sometimes have to ask them to go further than the more conservative members of their profession might go. Having a good enough relationship with each other to achieve this balance is important and a critical part of my job. A recent shoot provided an illustration of this.

By the middle of the final day at the 1998 live shoot at Bawsey in Suffolk we had very little concrete evidence for dating some of the major features. Mick and the other archaeologists were reluctant to open up more trenches, but by arguing the case and showing them the latest geophysics we were able to agree on two final trenches. These turned out to be crucial to our understanding of the site. In one we found dating evidence, including a beautiful loom weight, from the Anglo-Saxon period which at last gave us a date for the huge ditch that surrounded the site. In the other we uncovered an important set of Anglo-Saxon kilns that will prove vital to the future interpretation of what was happening at Bawsey 1,500 years ago. Without this information the site and the programme would have been poorer.

On the other hand, with my archaeological hat on I also have to ensure that the process of getting a programme made does not distort the archaeological reality. This can mean that the story line in a script that has been worked on and researched for weeks may have to be abandoned or I have to help by pushing directors down an entirely new path. If this does not happen I always feel that we must be going down a line that is too predictable. A viewer told us that he had overheard a group of students laying bets with each other on whether *Time Team* would find anything in that evening's programme, and it would be nice if this story were true. For me, pursuing the honesty of that uncertainty has been an important element in what makes the series work. It is why the programme is unique on television and I would like to think that this is one of the reasons for *Time Team*'s success.

Time Team has always faced the prospect of failure; we test a hypothesis and sometimes we get it wrong and have to think again. As usual, the sites described here took us on a roller-coaster ride from fear of failure to hopes of final success. *Time Team* is archaeology as it happens and I hope this book will enable you to share the traumas and struggle behind the cameras – the other half of the story that you don't always see in the final cut.

The Beginning

Time Team started with a book and a conversation. The book, left at my house by some friends, was *Fieldwork in Local History* by W.G. Hoskins. Its theme – that the landscape can be 'read' and that this reveals the past – fascinated me. So did Hoskins' readable style and his ability to introduce an interpretation of the landscape that brings it alive so that it can be appreciated by non-experts. At about this time a reservoir was being built in a valley to the north of Dartmoor. This involved flooding many ancient farm sites but before they were destroyed archaeologists would have the chance to uncover their early origins. Researchers in the area had for some time been convinced that the sites might go back to the Saxon period and earlier, but modern-day occupation and the tendency to convert ancient barns into dwellings meant that few had been excavated to any depth. I wrote a brief outline for a programme and sent it to Channel 4. The idea of a reservoir slowly filling with water, as excavators battled to find out what they could from sites that were gradually disappearing, seemed to strike a note with Sue Shepherd, the commissioning editor who commissioned three programmes.

With the help of Simon Timms, Devon county archaeologist, I began to work on the series, which was eventually called *Time Signs*. Simon introduced me to Mick Aston from the University of Bristol, and Mick in turn suggested Phil Harding to do some reconstruction archaeology. I had wanted to re-create some aspects of prehistoric life in the valley – the origin of the *Time Team* reconstructions or 'cameos' – and Phil showed us how to fell trees with a flint axe, create fire with a bow drill and make and shoot an arrow. I have fond memories of one of my first meetings with Phil. I had brought him down to the valley to demonstrate the use of a flint axe. We needed to film a sequence showing how prehistoric people cleared the forests. With camera rolling and amid an air of tense expectation Phil stepped up to a tree, swung his axe and delivered a mighty blow – only for the axe-head to drop out of the shaft. I think this was the first occasion on which I heard the immortal words 'Oh bugger!'. It became clear over the following months that despite the occasional mishap, Phil was not only a genius

Opposite: Professor Mick Aston meditating on the likely identity of an archaeological artefact – in this case a ship's nail. The striped pullover is standard Aston apparel.

in the area of flint knapping but was also prepared to have a go at a variety of ancient techniques in front of the camera.

Phil's skills and easy manner had an obvious appeal, and it was clear to me that Mick was a great communicator of archaeology. He described me as one of the few 'television people' – a derisive term in Mick's vocabulary – he could get on with and someone who, in addition, was prepared to read enough background material to understand what he was talking about. A friendship began.

Over a year and a half Phil, Mick and I traipsed up and down muddy valleys and helped to carry cameras and sound gear. Initially our cameraman was Bernard Hedges. Limited budgets and the need to record developments on the site at short notice meant that I was also doing camera work, and for the later programmes Bernard and I were joined by Nick Dance. Nick was to become the senior *Time Team* cameraman and his style of shooting, which reflects the way I want to capture archaeology 'as it happens', is a distinctive element in the series.

Opposite: *Anyone who has worked on* Time Team *knows it is an enjoyable experience – if hard work. Sue Francis agreed to help out with a cameo by rolling wool on her thighs. Damian Goodburn and Phil took a professional interest in the process.*

Above: *Victor Ambrus draws a picture of what the site may have looked like in the past. His drawings always prove a great attraction to the viewers and the local people. His ability to re-create the past in a short space of time under difficult circumstances is a unique skill that is a vital element in the programme.*

Above: *A typical place for a* Time Team *chat: around the bonnet of the Discovery. Nick Dance films Tony and Mick in conference with the experts.*

He is excellent at capturing the action and being in the right place to follow its thread. When we work with archaeologists, who are not actors, we have to get spontaneous reactions where possible, and capture the feel of a live-action sequence. Some cameramen shoot in short takes which need to be assembled in the editing suite with a lot of edits and cutaways, and the end result tends to feel less 'realistic'. With Nick and all the regular *Time Team* camera crews we try to capture the flow of an event. It was a piece of luck to meet Nick as early as I did.

The conversation that inspired the *Time Team* series was with Mick. As the filming of *Time Signs* progressed he and I began to enjoy discussing archaeology and after one filming day, wet, tired and in need of a cup of tea, we were chatting in a service station on the edge of the A30 near Dartmoor. Mick told me how he and a friend had missed a bus somewhere in the Midlands and spent an enjoyable hour waiting for the next one by mapping out the medieval streets of the town. My reaction was that if they could do that in an hour, how much more could be done in three days? *Time Team* was under way. Over the following six months

I put together different variations on the theme and included a 'cameo' reconstruction element.

Developing an initial idea into a successful television format requires a lot of hard work and trial and error. I wanted to put together a team of people with the right chemistry and set of ideas to carry the viewer along. Drawings by Victor Ambrus, whose illustrations had caught my eye in a second-hand Reader's Digest book on history, were included. With the introduction of an incident room, the historical reconstructions and the history sequences, that found their natural presenter in Robin Bush, the key features of the series were in place. At some point in the past Mick had held a course on archaeology in Greece which had been attended by one Tony Robinson, and Tony's interest in the subject and his connection with Mick made him an obvious choice for presenter. As a result of his experience in television he would also be a valuable source of advice as the series progressed. During a recent conversation with him he told me that nowadays more people come up and talk to him about his *Time Team* work than refer to his role as Baldrick in *Blackadder*.

An interesting element of the programme style is that from the beginning we decided that only Tony should address the camera: it is a television convention that viewers like to have just one person talking to them. Mick had done a great job in this role on *Time Signs* but he had to change his way of getting information across for *Time Team*. His good relationship with Tony was important in achieving the right chemistry. Tony could play the grit in the archaeological oyster and ask questions the viewers would like to ask. He would also be able to spot archaeological prevarications and generally keep the team on their toes. Field archaeologist Carenza Lewis completed the original team, joining us after the pilot.

After a year's wait due to changes in personnel at Channel 4 – 'You'll have to wait and see what the next commissioning editor thinks' – *Time Team* was under way. Karen Brown, our new commissioning editor, recognized its potential even though it was based

Above: *Somewhere in an English field, John, as on many occasions, explains the details of the geophysics results. Geophysics has become a crucial element of Time Team.*

on a subject that not many people would have thought of as popular viewing material, and the idea was presented to her by a producer who did not exactly have a typical television background.

In the waiting period *Time Team* had a brief existence as a spin-off – a sort of 'spot the object' game show complete with spinning panels – but it was always clear that the basic idea was strong and that, as *Time Signs* had shown, there was an audience for archaeology. The series had two other allies at Channel 4: John Willis and Andrea Wonfor who kept the idea alive while we waited for Karen Brown to take up her post.

From the start I wanted *Time Team* to be different from other history and archaeology programmes on television. I had watched many *Chronicles* and other history/archaeology programmes over the years and often enjoyed them, but I was suspicious of what I felt was a 'talking head' style combined with a sense of experts talking down to the audience. I knew real archaeology was about testing a hypothesis and often finding out that your initial guess was incorrect. I wanted a group of people who would take risks and get it wrong and still be able to keep going. I believed this would keep the programme always fresh.

It is to the great credit of all the team members that they were prepared to risk this approach when they were still uncertain whether or not *Time Team* would be accepted by their peers. They are among the rare group of archaeologists who have been prepared to stick their heads over the parapet to make the subject more popular to the general public. The extent of that popularity can be measured by the millions who watch the programme, and by other factors including the estimated fifteen per cent increase in applications to study archaeology at university, which many admissions tutors put down to *Time Team*'s influence. We have also received tremendous support and acceptance from the archaeological community and been awarded the British Archaeological Award for Best Archaeological Programme twice in a row. It is this kind of recognition that has helped to encourage our archaeologists.

Eight years after that first series went out, one of my great pleasures has been to remind Mick at regular intervals of his final words to me – the words of a good old Brummie cynic – when we parted at the service station after that initial conversation: 'It'll never happen Tim – it'll never happen.'

Below: *The directors on* Time Team *have to be flexible and cope with sudden changes to the script. It is my job to keep them aware of the likely direction the archaeology is going. Here Simon Raikes and I are discussing our strategy on Day Two of the Cheddar shoot.*

Who's Who

Tony Robinson, the series presenter, is best known for his role as Baldrick in *Blackadder* and as the Sheriff of Nottingham in *Maid Marian and Her Merry Men*, which he also wrote. He has a keen interest in history and archaeology – he is president of the Young Archaeologists' Club – and is particularly fascinated by ancient Greece and the biblical lands of the Middle East.

Professor Mick Aston, the team leader, has been involved with archaeology for more than thirty years, and is currently Professor of Landscape Archaeology at the University of Bristol. He has written numerous articles and books, including *Interpreting the Landscape*, the standard work on landscape archaeology.

Phil Harding works as a field archaeologist with Wessex Archaeology, and has been involved in a project listing and plotting all known Palaeolithic sites in Britain. He has also completed a number of excavation reports – including some for *Time Team* – on sites ranging from the Palaeolithic to the Industrial Revolution. He continues to demonstrate flint knapping at craft shows and to local societies.

Carenza Lewis has been with the Royal Commission on the Historical Monuments of England (RCHME) since 1985. A specialist in the medieval period and in historic landscapes, she worked extensively as a field archaeologist in Wessex and co-edited a collection of essays on the medieval landscape of this area; she is now based in Cambridge. Her book on the medieval landscape of the East Midlands – *Village, Hamlet and Field* – was published in 1997.

Victor Ambrus, who arrived in Britain from Hungary in 1956, is a freelance illustrator with almost 300 books to his credit. Winner of the World Wildlife Award and twice winner of the Kate Greenaway gold medal for the best illustrated book of the year, his recent work includes illustrated editions of *The Iliad* and *Moby Dick* and a book on the Anglo-Saxon ship burials at Sutton Hoo. He is a Fellow of the Royal Society of Arts and the Royal Society of Engravers.

Robin Bush, formerly deputy county archivist for Somerset, is a freelance lecturer, historian and broadcaster. An expert in genealogy and on the history of early emigration to the United States, he is the author of numerous books on local history, including a definitive guide to Somerset.

Stewart Ainsworth trained as a surveyor before moving into the archaeology section of the Ordnance Survey Department as an investigator, working in Britain on archaeological sites and monuments and, on secondment, on a mapping project on the Caribbean islands of St Kitts and Nevis. In 1985 he joined the Royal Commission on the Historical Monuments of England as an archaeological investigator and is now head of the field archaeology office for the West Midlands. Along with Bernard Thomason he is responsible for what we call the 'lumps and bumps'.

Bernard Thomason first worked in archaeology in 1972, as an air-photograph interpreter at Cambridge University. In 1980 he began working with the Royal Commission on the Historical Monuments of England as an archaeological illustrator. Since then he has been employed as an architectural surveyor and illustrator. He specializes in producing technical solutions to surveying and illustration, and is Head of Technical Survey for Archaeology at the RCHME.

John Gater has been involved in archaeological geophysics for almost twenty years, working for British Gas, the Ancient Monuments Laboratory (English Heritage) and Bradford University Research. In 1986 he set up GSB Prospection, an independent consultancy in geophysics for archaeology. He is also an associate editor of the *Journal of Archaeological Prospection*.

Dr Chris Gaffney has worked in geophysics since 1983, including extensive site-based experience in the United Kingdom, Greece and the former Yugoslavia. In 1989 he formed a partnership with John Gater at GSB Prospection. He too is an associate editor of the *Journal of Archaeological Prospection*.

Creative TV is responsible for *Time Team*'s computer graphics. **Sue Francis** worked with the BBC for two years and as a freelance designer before, in 1989, setting up Creative TV Facilities where she is chief designer. **Steve Breeze** was signed to RCA Records as a singer/songwriter before joining Creative TV where he creates three-dimensional visualizations.

The Production Process

Each series of *Time Team* begins with a huge pile of letters – we get more than a thousand a year – from members of the public, special interest groups concerned with protecting our history and, increasingly, archaeologists. We also have an idea of the kinds of sites we would like to go to because they have not appeared in previous series. Gradually a few start to establish themselves. Researchers reduce the pile by eliminating the weakest or frankly potty suggestions and begin to discuss sites that appear to be possible with people like county archaeologists.

I am often asked which kind of proposals make it through the system and which don't. The answer is partly the obvious one; that a letter accompanied by good drawings and photographs, and with some solidly researched archaeological content, is more likely to be accepted. Sending us bits of supposed archaeological material is not a good idea. In the past we have received interesting Roman necklaces that turned out to be lavatory chains and pieces of gravel that the punter was convinced bore the faces of Roman emperors.

It is very useful for us to know exactly who owns the land. Many great ideas fall by the wayside because we can't be sure that the landowner will allow us access. Often the research team will consider a relatively simple idea that has some good artefact evidence checked by a local archaeologist. In the 1998 filming year we carried out an excavation in a back garden in Papcastle, Northumbria. A family had uncovered a large number of Roman finds while building a patio there. They had made a careful inventory of their finds, got the local

archaeologist and museum to confirm that they were Roman and then sent us a letter complete with photographs of the site. This one belongs to a group we refer to as 'back garden punter' sites – a 'punter' is the name we give to a person who suggests we come to a site in the first place. We like to have at least some of this sort of punter in each series.

It is amazing how many people uncover important archaeology in their back gardens. The millions of gardeners happily planting their borders are potentially the largest group of field walkers we have. It is also surprising that so many of them discover finds which they feel won't be of interest to their museum or local archaeologists, but then decide to tell *Time Team* about them.

We are always on the lookout for places that viewers would not normally connect with archaeology, and like to have a variety of historical periods and archaeological environments. There is also an element of serendipity and experience. After forty programmes I have come to trust my instinct that a site is right and tend to follow my hunches. However, I am reluctant to go ahead if Mick, who is a useful source of contacts and ideas, has a strong reason for being against a site. Tony is kept informed of the kind of areas we are looking at and so are Channel 4 and Philip Clarke, the executive producer. An executive producer's job is to act as a sort of *éminence grise*, keeping an eye on both the administration of the programme and the direction it is taking. Any small company that comes up with a potentially successful idea tends to get pushed in the direction of a good executive producer, and Philip became involved with *Time Team* from Series 2 onwards.

A major part of my job is to make sure the right sites are selected. The choice tends to be my final decision – which can be a bit nerve-racking at times.

County archaeologists are one of our key groups of contacts. We have good contacts in most areas of the country and this has created an important network, which acts as a reference point when we begin to look for new sites. Our access to a site is often based on our ability to provide resources that would not otherwise be available. Geophysics is particularly useful and we often use it over a larger area than is actually necessary in order to supply data for local archaeologists. In Navan, County Armagh in Northern Ireland, they are still processing the work that the geophysics team did two years ago and excavating areas of interest based on the data.

Opposite: *Now I have worked with him for several years, Phil Harding occasionally allows me to have the odd scrape. Getting as close as possible to the archaeological reality is an important part of my role as producer – at least that's what I tell Phil.*

We are very dependent on county archaeologists or their equivalents and will not do a site unless we have their support. They are usually keen to know certain things before we start:

Who will be the archaeologist in charge? The answer is usually that it will be a local person from the county unit.

Who will be writing up the site? Report writing is a major concern to archaeologists and in many areas a moratorium has been declared on excavations until the backlog of reports has been cleared. It is essential that knowledge about sites is made available: information from a *Time Team* dig could be the last piece in a jigsaw and solve an archaeological mystery. Detailed drawings and photographs of all the stages the trenches pass through and detailed reports on the finds are essential. It is often necessary to call in an expert to evaluate the material. We allocate a sum of money in our budget for this – Mick refers to it as our archaeological insurance policy.

The situation is made more critical when we apply for scheduled monument consent. This means that the government, with advice from English Heritage, has given legal protection against disturbance and unlicensed metal detecting to a nationally important site or monument by adding it to a list or 'schedule'. Scheduling is a very strong piece of legislation that has to be respected and English Heritage has a team of people whose job it is to protect key sites of archaeological interest throughout the country. There are some 30,000 of these ranging from prehistoric standing stones and burial mounds to Roman forts, medieval villages and some more recent structures such as collieries and Second World War pill-boxes. Excavating on a scheduled site requires approval from the Secretary of State for the Environment and is a major event for us. We have excavated on two so far: Malton in North Yorkshire in Series 4 and the Beauport Park site in Sussex described in this book. Access is granted only if it can be shown that we will follow a set of guidelines – a 'research design' – and that we will write up our finds.

The research design specifies exactly how many trenches we can excavate and where, and specifies our goals and the personnel involved. It is one of the most useful documents at this stage and forms the basis of my discussions with the director as to the likely course of the programme. It also allows us to identify the specialist equipment and experts we will need which enables the production manager to draw up a budget. Many of our extra costs tend to be the result of unexpected technical problems caused by factors that were not predicted in the research design.

Once a site has been located and the research design formulated, the production team goes into action booking crews, hotels and organizing catering, travel and all the other elements that make a shoot run smoothly. Production manager Zarina Dick, co-ordinator Malaine Kegg, secretary Katy Segrove and Unit manager Alex Cox often have just two to three weeks to get everything in place. A *Time Team* shoot can involve over fifty people all of whom need accommodation and must be looked after at the site, which can have limited facilities.

We now have an additional member of the archaeological team: Peter Bellamy, whose sole job is to write up the reports on each site. We are keen to make sure all the sites we dig are well documented, including detailed geophysics reports from John Gater and Chris Gaffney and the location of trenches from Bernard Thomason and Stewart Ainsworth.

Above: In the incident room. Stewart Ainsworth uses the computer to sort out the landscape.

It is important that this information is made available to archaeologists in general and that our work is accurately recorded, particularly with regard to the position of the trenches. Bernard and Stewart use a Leica Global Positioning System (GPS) which relies on information beamed down by a constellation of twenty-four satellites belonging to the United States Department of Defense. These orbit constantly around the earth and signals can be received from at least four of them at any time of the day or night. By using sensitive equipment that can receive and decode the signals it is possible to get a very accurate three-dimensional fix anywhere in the world. With this technique trenches, geophysics grids, environmental bore-holes and field-walking can be accurately located on a map. GPS equipment

Behind the Scenes at *Time Team*

also enables Bernard and Stewart to record three-dimensional points and computerize them to create landscape models and a picture of what the site originally looked like. I am always amazed at how accurate the system is. It can locate a point in plan within three centimetres (1¼ inches) anywhere on the earth's surface. Theoretically a teacup outlined on one of our sites in Britain could be paid a visit by a missile flown from another continent.

Bernard makes a complete computerized record of the trenches and finds and our resident digging team also records trenches with a theodolite. Each key trench-level is drawn by hand using a grid suspended over the surface. Hand drawings are uniquely accurate recordings of a surface and are preferred to photographs.

The final question county archaeologists usually raise is: 'What about post-excavation and who'll make good?' Post-excavation covers a wide range of activities including writing up reports, processing finds and making sure the site is tidy and safe after we leave. On some shoots we have hundreds of finds to process. This includes cleaning, categorizing and, in the case of the more fragile ones, conserving them. Costs for this can run into thousands of pounds which might explain the somewhat ambiguous attitude I occasionally have to heaps of finds coming out of the trenches. A significant Anglo-Saxon burial with bones, grave goods and other artefacts could produce a bill in excess of £4,000 or £5,000 in the post-excavation stage. This has to be allowed for in the overall budget for a series.

An important part of the early stage of production is locating the incident room. This is where we have the computer equipment, books and maps and where we process finds. We also try to give Sue Francis and Steve Breeze an idea of the kind of structures they will be re-creating with their computer graphics, and let Victor know which historical period he needs to think about in advance. Victor's experience and skill mean he is able to give us an accurate drawing of a typical Saxon hut or medieval castle in a relatively short space of time. His

TIME TEAM SERIES VI
BEAUPORT PARK, EAST SUSSEX
Day One, Friday 19th June

CAMERA 1

*Above: After the script is
finished, each day's shooting
is mapped out on a schedule.
This tells the Time Team who
is filming what, where and
when. After a hard day's
filming the director has to
work on a new one for the
next day so they're not always
as neat as this.*

drawings are always a great attraction for the local punters and viewers alike and, combined with Sue's reconstructions of objects and Steve's three-dimensional buildings and landscapes, form a critical element of a programme.

Before a *Time Team* dig takes place we come to an agreement with the community as to where to send the finds. Often this is to the local museum. Landowners theoretically have the right of ownership but we usually persuade them to pass on any finds to an appropriate local body who will care for them. Any gold or silver object that has been hidden and whose owner is unknown is covered by the law of treasure-trove: it belongs to the Crown and is subject to an inquest at a coroner's court to establish the circumstances of its loss or deposition. Archaeologists frequently give evidence to such inquests. The person who has found the object is often allowed to keep it – or an institution like the British Museum may buy it for their collection.

Throughout this process Ella Galinski and Tory Batten, the assistant producers, make sure the archaeological story and programme narrative are accurate and that we are establishing good links with the community and experts. With so much investment of energy and money going into just three days it is critical that they – and the whole team – have a complete understanding of what we will be doing and that this is how the director sees the programme going. They work with the director on the likely route of the archaeology and it is then up to them and the researchers to visualize how the three days will be shot and produce a shooting script. The script includes details of Tony's pieces to camera and the order in which scenes will appear. It allocates a series of events to each of the main days and divides the presentation of the material between the various *Time Team* members. This document and the research design form the basis of a production meeting held a couple of weeks before the shoot, which is attended by everyone involved in the programme and enables us to get feed-back from the *Time Team*, Tony and the rest of the production team.

Below: Phil gets the chance to drink his favourite drink from a somewhat classier container than his usual pint glass.

CHAPTER 1

Cooper's Hole, Cheddar

TONY'S PIECE TO CAMERA: 'It may not look very comfortable, but before huts and houses this was home. In fact, this cave in the Cheddar Gorge could be one of the oldest homes in the country. Between five and ten thousand years ago families of Stone Age hunter-gatherers, the cavemen of legend, probably used this cave as a place to eat, sleep, shelter, and ... do whatever else they did. But to find whatever they left behind is going to be a huge task. Thousands of years of rainfall have washed tons and tons of mud into this cave, and washed much of the evidence deep into the tunnels at the back ... if we're going to find anything at all we're going to have to dig a long way down that way (*points down*), and a long way (*indicating tunnels*) that way ...'

Opposite: *Placing locating points for mapping the cave interior was an important element of ensuring that the finds and our trenches could be accurately located.*

Above: *Gathered together on the first day, Dr Larry Barham and Dr Kate Robson-Brown discuss tactics with Phil and Carenza.*

The Upper Palaeolithic Period

The Upper Palaeolithic period ran from *c.*40,000 BC to *c.*12,000 BC and is a key period in human history because it was a mini-Renaissance in our evolution. What could be called artistic or cultural developments occurred at this time – we are all familiar with the beautiful cave paintings produced by our Upper Palaeolithic or Stone Age ancestors – and new techniques for using flint were introduced. The change in flint technology that played a key role was that it was used for blades. These were made by striking fragments of stone from a core of flint and could be used as a basis for a number of tools. The introduction of blades was accompanied by a standardization of the basic components of tools and the development of composite ones. Making these involved gluing flint blades to wooden handles, usually with a combination of wood resin and beeswax. Along with more sophisticated tools, it is likely that there was a change in hunting techniques: we know from the contents of cave sites that a wide range of animals were hunted including deer and horse.

Some of the most important sites of the Upper Palaeolithic period in Britain are in the Mendip Hills of Somerset. These include Badger's Hole, which is part of the Wookey Hole complex and was excavated in 1938; Soldier's Hole in the Cheddar Gorge area excavated in 1928; and Gough's Cave, part of the Cheddar

Gorge complex excavated in 1904. The other major area in Britain is at Cresswell Crags in Derbyshire where Robin Hood Cave, Pinhole Cave and Mother Grundy's Parlour are of particular interest. Badger's Hole, Robin Hood Cave, Mother Grundy's Parlour and the Gough's Cave complex are particularly important because human remains have been discovered there. Gough's Cave, named after the excavator Richard Gough, yielded some of Britain's most important Stone Age archaeology including a skeleton of (Mesolithic) Cheddar man; one of the oldest and most complete yet found, it is over 9,000 years old. Recent research by Dr Chris Stringer of the Natural History Museum, London, suggests that he was in his forties when he died from a blow to his skull. He was discovered in 1903 by one of Richard Gough's sons.

It is worth remembering that not all our Stone Age ancestors lived in caves. Hengistbury Head in Dorset is an example of a late Upper Palaeolithic site where the occupants lived in the open landscape. Large amounts of flint were found there, but there was no sign of structures. Nick Barton, the archaeologist who excavated the site, used the technique of 'refitting' to show that the large range of flint objects scattered throughout its many layers belonged to the same period. This required great skill and patience and involved searching through the flints to locate pieces that belonged to one original core. Refitting is valuable for discovering the likely location of flint knapping activity.

The beauty of Palaeolithic caves is that they can hold evidence of our earliest experiments with art and ritual. Those in France and Spain contain beautiful cave paintings and in some cases stone and ivory carvings have been found. Sites around the Dordogne include Abri Pataud, La Madeleine, Laugerie-Haute, La Ferrassie and Lascaux.

F ive weeks before we were due to start filming in Cooper's Hole I received a call from an archaeology professor at one of our largest universities: 'Tim you shouldn't be doing this site – it's a bridge too far for *Time Team*. It's an incredibly important site that might have national importance.' Three days later I received an 'expression of concern' from the county archaeologist and a letter from Mick saying he was 'worried'. Programme Five of the 1998 filming year was already attracting the attention of the archaeological community.

The object of their attention was a rather unloved cave in the main Cheddar Gorge area. Unnoticed for years by visitors to the nearby Gough's Cave, this neglected corner of British prehistory had become a dumping ground for bits of old car, drinks cans and the occasional dead sheep. The only people who had shown any interest were a bunch of cavers determined to head their way into the nether regions, and a party of boy scouts who had enjoyed several holidays tunnelling into the mud.

The reason for the alarm generated by our interest in Cooper's Hole was the importance of the Upper Palaeolithic period and the relative scarcity in Britain of evidence from this time. We know that early man occupied caves in Cheddar Gorge – though not necessarily all of them – and human remains as well as bones from prehistoric meals had been found in Gough's Cave. The question was, would Cooper's Hole have any evidence of Stone Age occupation – human bones, for instance, or flint tools? If it did, that would be a major discovery.

I had been fascinated for some time by the idea that if you look at the skills we have used since our earliest days – when we had a brain approximately the same size as we have now – flint or stone technology has been dominant for ninety-eight per cent of the time. A large number of our flint-bashing ancestors would have inhabited caves not dissimilar to Cooper's Hole. Caves have the virtue of being strong structures that maintain a relatively consistent temperature throughout the year. They can be easily heated and are easily defended because attack from the rear is impossible. They are often located in sites that provided a good vantage point for watching potential prey. Sitting above Cooper's Hole it was easy for me to imagine herds of horses and deer running along the valley below. Long-term occupation means that debris will accumulate on the floor of the cave and can build up to a depth of several yards. It includes evidence of tools used for food, remnants

of hearths and even pollen that has blown in from nearby plants. This can make caves an invaluable record of prehistoric life.

There is a fascination to exploring deep inside the earth, which we had touched on during our excavation of a prehistoric 'fogou' site at Boleigh in Cornwall in Series 3, where we had attempted to unlock the secrets of an Iron Age underground passage, and early in the year I had discussed a number of possible prehistoric cave sites with David McComish of the Royal Commission on the Historical Monuments of Britain and Bob Croft, the Somerset county archaeologist. Bob suggested Cheddar Gorge as a possible location.

The mystery of British caves is that in the ones that have been uncovered there is no trace of the paintings and carvings found in French and Spanish caves. There is no clear answer as to why this should be. Were our ancestors less artistic than their French counterparts? Were they more interested in hunting mammoths? A researcher we were working with supplied an answer of sorts: 'taphonomy'. The explanation that followed had that air of complex scientific logic that is carefully constructed to hide the fact that no one has a clue.

The most likely reason is that climatic conditions made artistic activities less likely. Prehistoric men and women were too busy surviving to have time to create murals. Nevertheless, one would have thought that just one tiny sketch – even a doodle – would have made it on to a wall in the deep interior of what our ancestors called home. According to taphonomy, paintings did not survive because of the composition of the rock, but this seems unsatisfactory. Whatever the reason, the lack of artistic traces would make our search for Paleolithic people additionally difficult and we were left with bones and flint tools as the main targets for excavation.

The first step was to contact cavers and find out what exactly had happened in the 1960s and 1970s when they had first begun to explore the caves. Something of a sorry tale was revealed as a story emerged of ambitious endeavours, combined with a lack of concern for artefacts, that might be considered a little reckless. The fact that a possible Stone Age hand-axe had been found in Cooper's Hole, then lost on a bus after a heavy drinking session, was just one example! The cavers' disregard

Above: *Trench 1 underway in the car-park area. In the prehistoric period this might have been the main area of occupation. Some of the rock we began to encounter could have been fragments of roof.*

of *Time Team* removing layers of rubbish in order to make access to the cave easier. We had also raised the possibility of a second area of excavation outside the cave in an area close to the road. This involved clearance from the Somerset Highways Department and, because the trench might be deep, the need to contemplate a civil engineering job.

'Why dig outside the cave?' was the obvious question. The answer came from the experts. First, the cave roof has gradually been eroded away over the years so that the entrance today is much nearer the centre of the original cave than might appear. Second, our Stone Age ancestors spent much of their time at the opening to their dwellings. They would have been no keener than you or I to sit at the back of a smoky cave when there was sunshine at its entrance.

Larry and Kate had one more final condition. If we dug at the mouth of the cave we could go no further than a layer of clear archaeology, if one appeared. It is known that the caves were occupied from the Iron Age to Roman and later times, and we agreed that if we hit a layer of Roman archaeology we would not go through it because, like the stal, it might protect what lay underneath. This could, of course, mean that we would be unable to find the evidence of earlier periods that we needed.

By now we also had guidance from Andy Currant, who pointed out some salient facts. Evidence of occupation might go back fifty feet into Cooper's Hole; the bones of prehistoric horses and red deer found by R.F. Parry in the early 1930s indicated that the cave had been accessible in the Upper Palaeolithic (c.40,000–12,000 BC) period; and the stalagmite floor was like 'weak concrete and later occupation would not have damaged it, therefore Upper Palaeolithic layers might be protected underneath'. He also raised an interesting question: did Stone Age men and women eat each other? Evidence from Gough's Cave suggested a shortage of food and a cannibalistic diet. Would we find anything similar in Cooper's Hole? I have to say that the question in most of our minds at this stage was: would we find anything at all?

As Simon Raikes and I contemplated what there was left for us to excavate in Cooper's Hole, a negative view seemed to suggest that we were in for three days of hard work, with no certainty of achieving our goal. At this moment there is always the critical question of Tony's

Below: Tony, in full caving gear, prepares to head down into the depths. There are very few unpleasant situations he is not prepared to tackle on Time Team's *behalf.*

opening piece to camera (PTC). What will we hang our story line on? It is a bit like nailing your colours to the mast. Tony says something like, '*Time Team* has got just three days to find "X"'. Critical threads of the script hang on this and it commits us to ascertaining our line of attack. We don't like implying that we can find something when this is next to impossible. Equally, we don't like stating the obvious – the PTC has to be a challenge, a mystery, but the goal has to be attainable. What would it be for Cooper's Hole? Could we say: 'Will we find evidence of Stone Age man?' With some degree of reservation and trepidation we decided that this would be our angle. I say trepidation because I don't like Tony to carry a line like this, and feel we are selling the viewer an unachievable dream. There are too many archaeological television programmes that cynically propose a search for the lost ark or something similar, knowing there is no hope of finding it, but that it will grab the viewer's attention anyway. In the event, Tony's opening PTC stated that finding what Stone Age man left behind would be 'a huge task'.

We now had a strategy in place and after final telephone calls to Bob Croft and Lord Bath we could begin the countdown to filming. As we had all agreed that we would have to go as far as possible into the cave the cavers would be part of the team. Tony was prepared to go underground and we needed a cameraman who could cope with the technical challenge and a crew who would not mind getting muddy. Cameraman Clive North and *Time Team* sound supervisor Steve Shearn had had experience of caving and Clive had the technical know-how to ensure that we got pictures in this extreme environment. By now our researchers had come up with a chronology of events in the cave. This is a useful document for most sites and helps everyone to get a grip on what happened when.

According to at least one source a Mr Cooper was in occupation in the 1800s (apparently caves have always been popular places in which to live). Alternatively, and perhaps more likely, it was where he kept his cart – a convenient natural garage. In 1931 and 1932 excavations under R.F. Parry extended 4.5 metres (fifteen feet) into the cave and went down to 4.5 metres (fifteen feet). Parry found animal bones, layers of charcoal, an Iron Age layer and a layer of clay but possibly did not pierce the stal. Also in the 1930s, local cavers dug in the cave but found little. Bones claimed to be from the cave were donated to the Natural History Museum in 1946 and a fragment of the jaw of a red deer has recently been recorded as being from the lowest level (layer twenty) which looks

Above: Mick and Andy
Currant explore the recesses
of a cave-dweller's skull.
Some of the bones,
according to Andy, provided
evidence of cannibalism.

hours of filming began, we started to appreciate the realities of the challenge we had taken on. A rainy month previously meant surfaces were wet and the area of the cave where the stal had been broken was collecting water. Pumps could deal with some of this sea of liquid mud, but the only way to get rid of the handfuls of more solid clay and mud spoil that needed to be cleared was for a team of diggers and cavers to act as a chain gang to carry it to the surface. Rather like an underwater version of wartime escape movies, the team gradually worked it back in improvised plastic sleds which they dragged to the surface with ropes. The disturbed mud that had been washed over the top of the spoil had to be checked for artefacts and by the end of the day we had accumulated an interesting collection of drinks cans. We tried to work out how we could use a motorized winch but this had a major drawback – fumes from any vehicle would sink into the cave and, because the air in the shaft was already depleted by the number of cavers, would present a serious danger.

Trench 1 in the car park at the mouth of the cave had been started and was clearly going to be hard going. Trench 2 was deep down on the right-hand side of the cave in a tunnel that had been penetrated by cavers in the past. The combination of JCBs and heavy, mud-covered human diggers dripping rain and liquid mud created a fairly gruesome sight at the cave entrance, and as Day One came to a close it was with some relief that I contemplated a trip to the incident room to catch up on the story there. Mick Worthington, one of our key diggers, would keep an eye on things.

Andy Currant, our expert from the Natural History Museum, was able to give us the low-down on bits of bone which we had brought together in the incident room. He was able to elaborate on his theory that the bones in Gough's Cave a hundred yards down the road from our site showed evidence of cannibalism. One of the joys of *Time Team* is that in general we have access to the best experts going – the people who have done the most recent research and are familiar with up-to-date ideas on their subject. Andy was both an enthusiast and a great communicator. The only problem was that the longer we discussed what he had found in Gough's Cave, the more obvious the lack of evidence retrieved so far from Cooper's Hole became.

Below: *Lord Bath pays the team a visit and gets a view of the interior via our remote camera. Carenza was soon to enter the cave herself.*

Above: Expressions of concern, worry and fear as we contemplated the depth and instability of Trench 1.

It was one of the weekend's lighter moments when the Marquis of Bath decided to pay us a visit. As usual Mick, Phil and the rest of the team stopped to chat. Lord Bath was able to fill us in on the details of his genetic inheritance in comparison to that of his butler who, it turned out, was closer to Cheddar Man.

Over the weekend Lord Bath and his excellent staff were a great help and this kind of co-operation is critical to *Time Team*'s success. We would be stuck without the help of landowners, from farmers concerned about crops and cows to house-owners who want us to replace the patio in their back garden. The landowner is often the punter, and will have an interest in archaeology, but we always have to be sure that we have attended to the element of 'making good'. Bearing in mind that many *Time Team* trenches look like the Somme, it is necessary to convince the owner that we will put it all back again.

At an early shoot in 1995 at Lambeth Palace we were cheerfully digging up the Archbishop of Canterbury's grounds when he told us that the Queen would be at a garden party there in two weeks time. The mystery in all this is that there is always more soil than you could imagine, and it is harder to get it back in than dig it out.

Richmond Palace in Surrey (Series 6) presented the most difficult challenge. A pristine croquet lawn, an owner of fierce determination and one of London's first gardens reduced us to calling in professional help. The turf squares were removed by hand, watered lovingly and relaid by experts. A month later not a sign of one of our biggest excavations could be seen. One surprising fact is that farmland turf grows better if you stick it back soil upwards.

By the end of Day One our system for removing spoil from the cave was functioning smoothly but was proving a real test of the stamina of everyone involved. The surface team of spoil-searchers was still not having luck with finds.

Day Two saw Trench 1 in the car park reaching a dangerous depth, so much so that Mick and I became increasingly worried. We had hit a length of charcoal possibly washed down from further up the valley, but no earlier layers. At each stage we checked progress with Larry and Kate and sampled material from relevant layers. John's seismics produced good results and indicated a layer fifteen feet down which could be the bedrock. Seismics involves using a sledgehammer or small explosive charge to send a wave of energy wave into the ground. As the wave passes through the surface and the different layers there are distinct changes in its speed and at each interface some energy bounces back to the surface. The time it takes for this energy to travel from the surface into the ground and back again is recorded by a line of sensors (geophones) and this records the layers in a vertical section through the earth. The technique is similar to ground-penetrating radar (GPR) but unlike GPR, which is limited on 'wet' sites such as clay, seismics is best suited to the conditions we found at Cheddar.

The restricted space in the car park meant that the trench was approaching a

depth where we might not be able to step the sides to ensure that excavation would be safe. According to safety regulations, trenches more than 1.2 metres (four feet) deep require two possible actions: shoring, sloping the sides at a forty-five degree angle, battering or stepping the sides. Substantial barriers must be erected around excavations deeper than two metres (6½ feet). Stepping simply means widening the trench so that it can be dug down in a series of steps which make the sides more stable. Shoring is a critical business and, if lives are not to be endangered, must be carried out perfectly. A frame of metal or wood is inserted in the hole and prevents the sides collapsing. A trench never seems to be the best size for the accro props – adjustable steel tubes to support the shoring – you have on hand, which can cause delays while new ones are hired and the hole is shored to everyone's satisfaction. I have stood close to trenches when they have collapsed and the sound of the falling sides and the speed at which they fall is frightening. We always err on the side of caution once a trench approaches the magic depth of 1.2 metres (four feet).

Trench 1 created a panic, but it is difficult to say why. It was definitely deep and dangerous, but we had seen similar trenches before

Opposite: Some trenches just have an unpleasant look and this one was potentially lethal. However, we still had to measure its depth and try to record the layers prior to back-filling.

Above: Carefully perched near the edge of Trench 1, Dr Larry Barham points out some of the main features. After this final shot, and with recording of the main details complete, the trench was back-filled as the sides had started to collapse.

Above: *Phil carving the hole in the bone tool. At this stage we had yet to test its possible function.*

Opposite: *Flint knapper Phil in his natural element – working away at the mouth of a cave.*

and they had not produced such an air of worry among the diggers and the team. I think it is true to say that trenches have personalities. You look at a particular hole and it looks nasty and mean – the kind of hole that would bite your leg off. This had that sort of look – a bull terrier with attitude. People would come up to me, draw me to one side and gesture at it saying, 'It's a killer.' Mick became increasingly concerned and we all felt that we did not want anyone even near the edge. As bits of rock began to fall into the trench they landed on the bottom with a solid 'thunk' and you could feel the earth shake. We decided that our last act would be to measure the depth of the trench and backfill as soon as possible. Phil with a tape measure and Richard Trainer with digital machines miraculously managed to get the same reading – much to Phil's delight – and it gave us the level of the original rock surface outside the cave at which it had been during prehistoric occupation.

With the necessary safety precautions under way I was able to enjoy the more pleasant sight of Phil Harding doing what he does best: flint knapping. He first had to make the basic flint tool for the programme's cameo. This was a boring tool called a 'burin', a flint blade that has had a piece removed to create a ninety degree angle. With this

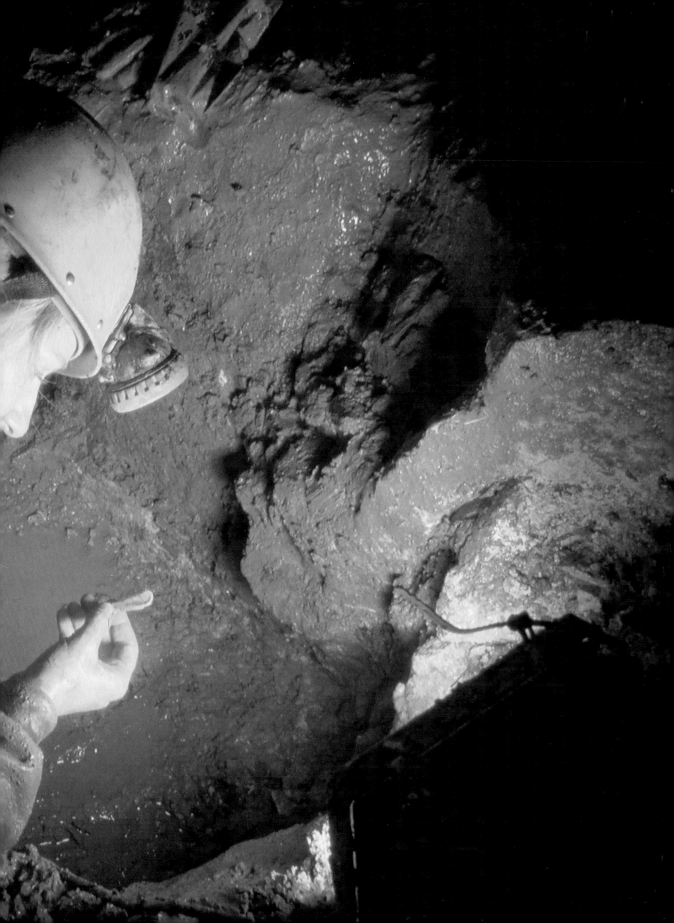

Previous page: Carenza, ten
metres (thirty feet) down and at
last in possession of what
might be a crucial piece of
evidence. The involvement of
the crews in the emotion of the
programme is something
special to Time Team.

Above: Relief and excitement at
the cave mouth after Andy
Currant identified the bone as
prehistoric. Carenza shares the
moment with our regular
soundman Steve Bowden.

he would make a *bâton de commandement*, one of the Upper
Palaeolithic period's most enigmatic objects. Two examples had been
found at nearby Gough's Cave. The term describes an object made from
antler horn, often with a hole pierced in its thicker end. Like all such
artefacts the *bâton* provides an ideal opportunity for academics to
theorize. Suggestions as to its use include that it was a lasso and that its
handle was used to gain extra purchase; that it helped climbers to
ascend and provided a brake when they descended; that it was a thong-
stropper to remove bits of flesh from leather thongs; an arrow
straightener and, most interestingly, a sex aid. (The last explanation was
suggested by my namesake Timothy Taylor, who has written an
intriguing book on the sexual element in archaeological finds. The fact
that we have the same name has often caused confusion. People come
up to me and say with interest, 'So you are Timothy Taylor' – to which
I have to reply, to their obvious disappointment, in the negative.) It
seemed clear that making the object would be fairly straightforward for

Phil but that, given this wide interpretation, demonstrating its use might present problems.

On Day Three we began to get deeper in Trench 3 in the left-hand corner of the cave where a tunnel had been widened by cavers, but blocked off by a subsequent rock fall. It was another important area for us because, once again in the right-hand tunnel the Stal had been penetrated in the past. Carenza in her full caving kit committed herself to going deep into the cave interior to see if anything could be found. With Trench 1 in the car park now closed down and Trench 2 rapidly filling with mud and water, Trench 3 became our last chance. In the early part of the day small pieces of bone had been seen here and Carenza had clearly located an area where cave deposits had accumulated. With all the mud and silt around, it was difficult to see whether it was under the stal or just close to it. As time ran out she finally located one piece of bone with cut marks on it. Andy Currant, to everyone's delight, confirmed they had been made by a flint tool.

Conclusion

In his final report Andy Currant wrote that the bones from Trench 3 tied in well with the material which had just turned up in the zoology department of the Natural History Museum, claimed to be from Parry's dig in the 1930s, but that he did not see anything which couldn't be Iron Age – sadly including Carenza's fragment with cut marks. All the butchery marks he could find on the Cooper's Hole material at the museum were also made with stone tools. He concluded: 'The long and short of it is that we didn't really get far enough below the stalagmite floor to stand much of a chance of finding anything convincingly Upper Palaeolithic, but given the restrictions we were working under I suppose that was inevitable. I still find it very strange that archaeologists should go to such lengths to prevent us from finding any archaeology.'

I would hope this still allows us to suggest that our bones may have been Upper Palaeolithic – we just can't prove it.

Below: What all the fuss was about – you can just make out the scratches created by a stone tool.

Following page: One of the cavers, myself, Simon Raikes and Mick Worthington with what one of our researchers called 'the remains of a prehistoric Kentucky Fried Chicken dinner'.

CHAPTER 2

Burslem, Stoke-on-Trent

TONY'S PIECE TO CAMERA: 'Everyone knows the name of Wedgwood when it comes to pottery, and this is what they have in mind: the blue and white design which is famous throughout the world. But few people know that it was here in Burslem, on the outskirts of Stoke-on-Trent, that Josiah Wedgwood's climb to fame and fortune first began. This is actually the site of his first factory, which was at the heart of the pottery industry as it took off in the eighteenth century. But does any of it survive under the paving stones of modern-day Burslem?'

Above: *Local archaeologist, Bill Klemperer, shows Mick and Tony an engraving of buildings from the time of Wedgwood's first pottery.*

Opposite: *Fragments of nineteenth-century pottery – just the tip of the iceberg of our cache.*

Pottery Production in Stoke-on-Trent

For centuries the hundreds of potteries scattered around the Stoke-on-Trent area were the main sources of Britain's china. It is usual to refer to the 'five pottery towns' but in fact there were six: Burslem, Hanley, Longton, Stoke, Tunstall and, the one that is often forgotten, Fenton.

Pottery production was one of the many processes that came together in the eighteenth century to create the Industrial Revolution. Stoke-on-Trent developed as a pottery centre because it possessed the necessary raw materials, the most important of which were coal to power the furnaces and clay which provided the raw material. There was also a skilled work force and a tradition of pottery making that went back more than a thousand years. Evidence that the Romans were the first to set up potteries in the area comes from a 1955 excavation at Trent Vale where a small circular kiln, pieces of cooking pots, 'face mask' jars with faces in relief and *mortaria* (similar to a pestle and mortar and used for the same purpose) were found. Pottery making was taken up again in the Middle Ages and excavations have shown that a local industry was thriving at this time. One of the most important medieval sites was at Sneyd Green near Burslem. Here excavators found a large amount of pottery material including green-glazed wares and quantities of 'Midlands purple', a highly fired dark-coloured pottery. The kilns at Sneyd Green also produced pottery and floor tiles for the monks at nearby Hulton Abbey. By the end of the seventeenth century, Burslem, the site of our excavation, was producing thousands of items of pottery.

Josiah Wedgwood, one of the pioneers of the Industrial Revolution, was born in 1730, one of twelve children. His parents were in the pottery industry and he learned his craft from his brother Thomas. When he was eleven years old he suffered from smallpox and as a result the lowest part of one leg was amputated. This meant that throughout his life one of his employees had to provide the muscle power to turn his pottery wheel.

In 1754 Josiah became a partner in the established firm of Thomas Wheildon and in 1759 he established the Ivy House Works in Burslem. The Etruria factory was opened in 1769. He was an enlightened employer for his time and provided housing for his workers. John Wesley preached in the potteries in 1760 and was clearly impressed with Wedgwood: 'I met a young man by the name of J Wedgwood who planted a flower garden adjacent to his pottery. He also has his men wash their

Behind the Scenes at *Time Team*

hands and face and change their clothes after working in the clay. He is small and lame, but his soul is near to God.'

Since the early eighteenth century, English potters had been attempting to reproduce the beautiful designs found on Chinese porcelain. Delftware made in Holland, London, Liverpool and other pottery centres featured blue, painted designs created by individual artists, but it was the popularization of transfer-printed earthenware in the 1780s that made highly decorated pottery affordable. The standard 'willow pattern' design originated in the Spode factory, but soon everybody was doing their own version. There are probably over a hundred variations and the Wedgwoods produced their own. This tendency to follow current artistic interests led to the manufacture of masses of blue-and-white ware which, archaeologists will tell you, seems to appear almost everywhere they dig in the Stoke-on-Trent area.

With industrialization, pottery making reached its peak in the mid-nineteenth century. It is estimated that at this time there were over 130 works in Burslem alone, employing approximately 20,000 people. The Wedgwood family made a significant number of innovations, not so much in the way that pottery was made but in how the manufacturing process was organized: they moved their potteries towards a production line system.

The potteries began to decline after the 1870s because of competition from other countries, notably the United States where American firms set up in business and the French developed a thriving market for porcelain and bone china. It has been estimated that over a third of 'five towns' pottery had previously been exported to America. During this century there has been an attempt to revive the industry, and this has resulted in the development of what might be called 'designer' or 'studio' pottery created by people like Clarice Cliff.

Above: *The interior of a kiln – plus stationary exhibit – shows the complex brickwork needed to create the roof structure.*

urslem was originally billed as the dig that would unearth Josiah Wedgwood's first kiln. The site was suggested by Bill Klemperer, Stoke-on-Trent's city archaeologist, and pursued with some tenacity by researcher Julian Hudson. Wedgwood's role as one of the key figures of the Industrial Revolution made his Ivy House Works a tempting target. However, it had been occupied by kilns for decades after his departure and its location in the centre of Burslem, now a part of Stoke-on-Trent, meant that I needed some convincing before we went ahead.

Urban archaeology has produced fascinating sites for the *Time Team* in the past, but they have been accompanied by the difficulties of digging in close proximity to a jumble of concrete, pipes and cables. I still have clear memories of some of the trenches we dug on the site of Matthew Boulton's mint in Birmingham in Series 4, where deep, unstable trenches were filled with brick rubble, piping for utility services and a large underground petrol tank that leaked fumes. The Wedgwood site raised some difficult questions. Would the substantial later buildings, including the neo-classical meat market, have buried or destroyed the site? Would we be able to tell the difference between an early Wedgwood kiln and the layers of later kilns? The deeper the researchers went, and the more information we began to accumulate, the more the site began to appeal to me.

We were dealing with a relatively narrow period of time. Wedgwood had occupied the site for less than four years, from 1759 to 1762. He had early declared, in a manner characteristic of the time, that he wanted to be 'pottery maker to the universe' and there were many similarities between him and Matthew Boulton. Both men were at the forefront of the Industrial Revolution. In their respective fields they developed methods of production that saw a massive increase in the output of two of our most basic objects: coins and household pottery. The transition from individual artisans creating unique artefacts that could often be traced to their particular style had been replaced by a world where mass production created thousands of identical objects in an unbelievably short time.

Wedgwood's desire to put decent, highly glazed pottery into every home was mirrored by Boulton's wish to provide everyone with coins that could not be counterfeited and were worth their face value. They both combined rigorous and energetic entrepreneurial skills with a social conscience, and saw the whole world as their potential market.

As with Boulton's factory, a plan of the Burslem site which would help us to locate individual buildings on the ground was a key piece of information. In more recent times it had been covered by a car park and a small square with trees, lawns and flowerbeds, plus seats and a bandstand. The area had been selected as the location of Ceramica, a community-based project, funded partly by the Millennium Commission, to restore Burslem's old town hall and the surrounding square and create a new pottery museum and heritage centre that would celebrate the history of the potteries. The project, initiated by local people, started in 1995 and it is expected that the museum, which will take into account the archaeology we found over the three days, will be completed and open to the public in 1999.

We knew that at an early stage in the filming it would be useful to show the archaeologists the kind of pottery to look out for, and a group of local experts selected some key pieces and placed them in chronological order. The imaginative designs with their different colours and shapes were an introduction to the variety of material we hoped to find.

The great virtue of pottery to the archaeologist is that it continually changes in style and that these changes can be dated. A series of pieces of pots or other artefacts, such as brooches or swords that can be placed in historical order, is called a typology. Each object has its date and therefore serves as a frame of reference for similar ones found at other sites. For us, one of the key types of pottery would be Wedgwood's creamware. We know from documentary records that it was produced at a certain date, and if it turned up underneath a layer of bricks we would know that the bricks had been laid after the last date for the first production of this style of pottery. Large amounts of creamware associated with one layer would be strong dating evidence. However, layers in a trench can be confusing.

The critical judgement is always whether or not we can be sure that an object comes from a particular layer, or has worked its way up or down from adjacent ones. In the trenches at Stoke-on-Trent there were layers of eighteenth-century buildings with nineteenth-century features cutting into them. Excavation in these circumstances has to be highly skilful to get an idea of the relative order of the material you are finding.

Mick often uses the analogy of eating a trifle to explain the point. If you dive straight into it and drag out the nice bits at the bottom – the archaeological equivalent of the pieces of sherry-soaked sponge –

Above: *Creamware: the key artefact linking our excavation back to Wedgwood pottery.*

Team Profile

Julian Hudson – *Researcher*

'I loved Wedgwood because of the sense of community that surrounded the shoot and the ease with which it seemed to work. I felt it was a job well done in true archaeological fashion.

'I was drawn to the aspect of 'how' we knew what we knew about the past at school, so after leaving I joined a local archaeology company as a volunteer digger and a year later went on to do a degree in archaeology. My first professional experience was as a site supervisor, followed by contractor after completing an MA in Archaeological Survey. In that time I went to Jerusalem for six weeks to do a 'Medieval and Ottoman Survey Project', which was tremendously exciting and allowed us privileged access to areas of the city.

'Getting into television from there was really a stroke of luck. I had been fascinated by the idea of working in the media for a while and made contact with an old friend who was working on a programme about dinosaurs for the Discovery Channel. Consequently I was taken on for five weeks' work experience in April 1996 and I left two years later to join *Time Team*, having become a researcher.'

Opposite: A visit to a complete kiln for comparison with the remains we were finding. As is often the case on Time Team, *the camera is hand held.*

everything gets mixed up. In an excavation, if you remove every layer carefully you stand a chance of working out what comes from each one and the order or chronology of the site. People who dig holes in pursuit of objects risk losing track of the layers or, to give them their archaeological label, contexts, and may remove the one critical artefact that would have dated a lower layer. It is a fairly regular occurrence that later activity on a site cuts through earlier contexts. For instance, on *Time Team* we have come across Roman sites with Anglo-Saxon pits dug into them. This perhaps helps to explain why archaeology can be so confusing – and, as Mick says, why it is always interesting to see how an archaeologist eats a trifle!

The particular trifle we were dealing with in Burslem soon duly produced some confused and interesting layers, and in Trench 1 we hit

Above: *Mick overlooks the site of Trench 1 where the JCB is well underway. The noisy traffic presented major challenges to our sound crew.*

the solid remains of the meat market which had been built in 1835 and demolished in 1957. A brick building with a stone façade, it had been twice the size of the adjacent town hall.

A large area of concrete sealed the surface and we needed heavy equipment to dig below it. Anyone who has hit concrete with a pickaxe will know that it is one of the construction industry's more unpleasant and solid inventions. A mechanical digger equipped with a concrete-breaker was necessary and we were lucky to have an expert to operate it. Kevin Grainger, a demonstration driver for JCB in Rochester, was on hand for the three days with a 3CX Backhoe loader.

I have watched skilled digger-drivers in action on many of our sites and seen how they arouse mixed emotions in archaeologists. However, to remove large amounts of sterile topsoil or urban rubble by hand is a waste of everyone's time and energy, and many sites would not be excavated if the work was restricted to hand digging. A good digger-driver can remove thin layers with great care and, with an expert holding a watching brief, most archaeologists would accept that this is perfectly sensible practice.

John and Chris had brought ground-penetrating radar which was needed to get through the tarmac covering the car-park site. This is being used ever more frequently in archaeology because it can provide detailed information about the depth and form of deposits. An electromagnetic field is transmitted into the ground and reflected back to the surface by buried features such as ditches, walls, etc. so that a series of vertical and horizontal slices through the ground can be viewed. He managed to get a response that could be the northern extension of the Ivy Works although we knew that a police station and air-raid shelter had been built in the area at a later date, after the pottery. A trench here became Trench 4.

Time Team has had mixed results with radar. In the early days a number of different companies tried to sell it as the answer to all archaeologists' prayers, almost as though there would be no need to dig any more. However, the reality was that we ended up with yards of attractive colour print-outs that never seemed to quite locate what had been expected. The reasons for this were bafflingly scientific. Added to

Below: *Heavy plant machinery in action. Urban archaeology can require severe measures.*

Above: Meeting the local diggers for a cup of tea before we start. We give them an outline of what we hope to achieve while thay give us useful background on the site.

Opposite: The director, Graham Dixon, holds a lightweight monitor and the soon-to-be-amended script. He keeps in contact with crew members via a microphone and earpiece.

the problem of failure to locate was the fact that you need a three-dimensional imagination to interpret the slices that radar produces. With resistance surveys or magnetometry you see the target in plan – that is, with good results the shape of a building emerges as though seen from above. In the last year our radar results have been more positive, possibly because our resident geophysics team have been operating the latest gear and have a better idea of how their findings need to be shown on screen. Geophysics results and landscape surveys all require processing time and the delay in getting an answer has to be built into the programme's schedule. I am endlessly asking John or Chris for an estimated time of arrival for the latest print-out. They in turn have to face the difficulties of operating computer gear in the field.

One of the big differences between *Time Team* excavations and many others that use geophysics is that we start digging relatively soon after the results have been interpreted. There is no delayed gratification. On conventional sites it is often years before trenches are dug which means that the geophysics team have to wait to calibrate their readings against the reality of what they see, before they can confirm the nature of similar readings elsewhere on the site.

By the end of Day One two trenches were open. Trench 1, the one nearest the road, revealed a rather nice Victorian tiled floor. In Trench 2, near the bandstand, there was an area of bricks that seemed to be made up of a number of layers. This was the first possible indication of a kiln but there was no pottery and no other dating evidence. The lower layer of brick looked much older than the one above. It was made of clay that seemed to contain a number of different-coloured elements as opposed to the more uniform body of the later bricks. There was also a structure that appeared to be a drain but might be part of the kiln cutting into the excavation. Interpreting this jumble of layers looked daunting, and the solid nature of the upper foundations made me concerned that the later building might have wiped out the earlier evidence we were looking for.

As usual our discoveries were beginning to conflict with the script – the key bit of paper with which we head into a *Time Team* programme – and Graham Dixon, the director, had to adjust to the reality of the finds in Trench 1 and Trench 2.

The likely route of the next day's archaeology has to be reflected in the schedule, which tells everyone what will be shot when. *Time Team* often works with three camera crews which can mean that a number of critical scenes are shot at the same time. In this case the director takes the main area, which usually involves Tony, and the associate producers and researchers are briefed to look after the other crews. I move between the three trying to judge where the archaeology is heading and when we need to change our plans to meet the next archaeological twist of fate. At Burslem we decided to concentrate more of our time on the material coming from Trench 2.

The other bit of paper that is often useful is an improvised plan of the site that shows the location of the trenches as they go in. Letting viewers know exactly where they are in relation to each one is always a concern and a site with several trenches can be confusing. The plan frequently makes an appearance on screen and we always try to have paper and large felt tip pens handy to allow Mick or Tony to sketch out the geography for the viewer. The crane shot, which gives an overhead view of the site, and which we have used increasingly in recent series, is also helpful.

Opposite: *On top of an increasingly large pile of pottery, I take five minutes to check where we are in the script and if it is matching the reality of the trenches. The sodden condition of the script was the result of a spectacular downpour.*

Above: *The glimpse of brickwork that gave us the first clue that we might be on top of an early kiln.*

work closely with the community we get relatively few problems on our shoots – but it is always a relief to have security guards, just in case.

Early on Day Two the spectators crowded around Trench 3 saw our diggers unearth a massive cache of decorated pottery – a fantastic sight. It dated from the 1830s – a period later than Wedgwood – and may have been one of a number of dumps intentionally left by Enoch Wood, a very important local potter who clearly, according to local legend, had a benign attitude to the archaeologists of the future and left 'time capsules' under public buildings.

The hoard we had uncovered illustrated the vast array of shapes and designs that were created in a relatively short space of time. Potters were attentive to the latest interests and fashions and when an exhibition of classical pots proved to be a great success in London, Josiah Wedgwood began to make reproduction Etruscan vases. Ironically, they were copies of Greek vases imported into Italy which eighteenth-century excavators had mistakenly identified as Etruscan. However, the line was so successful that he named one of his factories Etruria.

The cameo was now under way. We had decided to make a Wedgwood vase, and to get Victor Ambrus to draw a typical illustration. This was the most difficult element. It normally takes a trained pottery artist three days to produce a design and we had to make the pot, fire it and illustrate it in the same time. We had chosen creamware as our basic material. The enamels are mixed with linseed oil which means that they can smudge when painted on the pre-glazed surface. Victor gradually got the hang of working on a turntable and was able to complete the complex design in just a day. We used a mixture of a green and brown as these colours can be fixed at the same temperature.

By this time Trench 3's massive haul was of major interest to the pottery experts who took on the task of washing and, in some cases, fitting together bits of pot. Refitting requires Zen-like patience. One

Above: Trench 1 had evidence of a possible kiln and had already produced drinking vessels. The wire fence allows the public to see what is happening from a safe distance.

Opposite: Under orders from local pottery experts, Phil selects samples of the pottery hoard. This had been smashed at the time of burial and so some could later be stuck together to make almost complete pieces.

piece in particular, a rather fine chamber pot, had a highly unusual design that the experts thought was unique. As Victor's cartoon (page 87) made clear, Phil now had a pot to piss in!

Back in Trench 1 the Victorian floor was recorded, photographed and removed. Which layer is the one of key archaeological interest is often an issue, and someone had to decide to sacrifice the Victorian level in order to see what was below it. At Malton in North Yorkshire in Series 4 we stopped excavating the site of a possible Roman fort because we found a previously unrecorded set of Jacobean garden features above it. At Burslem the decision was easier because the site was due to be developed, which meant that most of the later areas of archaeology would be destroyed anyway.

With the Victorian floor layer well documented and photographed we could move on. Below it was a much earlier layer with pieces of early eighteenth century pot in the section. Small medallions containing the initials of Queen Anne and the dates of her reign, AD 1702–1714, were attached to some pieces of this brown ware, which was known as 'mottled ware', and measured the contents of the pots. One theory was that we might have been in the vicinity of an early pub,

CHAPTER 3

Beauport Park, Sussex

TONY'S PIECE TO CAMERA: 'This is the thirteenth fairway of a golf course in East Sussex, but just over there in the woods, a Roman bath house has been discovered. It's an incredible find, complete with underfloor heating, tiled floors, and walls which survive up to window height. But what is a Roman bath house doing here completely on its own, forty miles from the nearest Roman town? What was happening here 1,900 years ago?'

Opposite: Jake Keen begins our attempt to reproduce a furnace for melting iron. Local clay and straw are being compressed. Later they will be dried out by a slow-burning fire.

Above: Somewhere in the woods, under a camouflage of tin roofs and plastic, was a unique archaeological site from the Roman period.

The Romans in Britain

The army of the Roman Empire first set foot on British soil in 55 BC, led by Julius Caesar, but failed to gain a permanent foothold. This was left to the emperor Claudius who invaded Britain successfully in AD 43. His invasion force was said to have included a couple of elephants and I have always wondered whether their graves might be awaiting a *Time Team* dig somewhere in the south-east ... or did Claudius take them back?

Britain had an attractive set of natural resources for the Romans to exploit – iron, tin, gold and lead in abundance – and they mined these from the earliest days of occupation. Not surprisingly, the British were not delighted to be under the Roman yoke and most mining operations came under the command of the military. In one of the earliest *Time Team* programmes, at Rochester in Kent, we saw a reconstruction of a defensive ditch built by Roman legionaries. It was an effective demonstration of how civil engineering at the edges of the empire had to be undertaken by men who could defend themselves if necessary.

The Romans needed ironwork for swords, shield bosses and a wide range of military equipment. They also used iron farming implements and fittings in houses. There is some evidence that so much iron was made in the Weald that it was exported overseas. The baths at Beauport Park were found under a massive pile of iron slag, which had clearly come from a major ironworking site.

Bath houses are fascinating structures and symbolize the Romans' desire for civilised facilities even in this far-flung edge of the Empire. They were part of the social life of the Roman Empire, not just places for getting clean in, and bathing involved an elaborate ritual. When a Roman official retired to one of them he put his clothes in a 'locker' in the changing room, the *apodyterium*, near the entrance, and plunged into a cold pool in a room called the *frigidarium*. He then moved on to a warm pool in the *tepidarium* and, finally, a hot one in the *caldarium*. Here his body was oiled, often by slaves, and his skin was scraped with a *strigil* – a blunt blade that removed oil and dirt. There was often an exercise area and a place where bathers could relax after a final plunge in the cold pool.

To exist at all, bath houses needed sophisticated building techniques and efficient channelling of natural resources. A complex system of plumbing distributed warm and hot water to the pools in the *tepidarium* and *caldarium*. The rooms themselves were kept at the required temperatures by furnaces that sent hot air through a series of hollow pipes under the floors and in the walls – without

releasing deadly waste gases. The Romans developed waterproof cement, *opus signinum*, for the floors. These were suspended and often decorated with mosaics, which required vast numbers of tiles and skilled builders to lay them. The box-flue tiles with their distinctive scored surfaces that provided a key for plaster are one of the most easily recognizable clues to the existence of a bath house. In the case of the Beauport Park site a number of roof tiles had been found stamped with the letters CL-BR. This identifies them as belonging to the imperial fleet in Britain, the *classis Britannica*, the seaborne wing of the Roman army whose officers were also in charge of iron production.

Above: *Local amateur archaeologists point to the areas of previous excavations while Guy de la Bédoyère, Carenza and I try to make sense of it all.*

At Beauport Park near Battle in Sussex we were dealing with one of the best preserved, standing Roman buildings in southern England. Walls up to 2.4 metres (eight feet) high with window ledges make it a unique site. It also has 'lockers' where bathers kept their clothes. These have been found intact in only a few other sites in Europe – the bath house at Chesters (the Roman Cilurnum), on Hadrian's Wall, Pompeii, Herculaneum and two sites in Spain. They have also been found in Herod's bath house at Masada in Israel.

Although the site is close to the Beauport Park golf club the owners of the club were interested and helpful, and took the view that archaeology might attract tourists. However, we agreed not to dig up the golf course if this could be avoided. The site is surrounded by woodland and a small stream runs through it. Scheduling would restrict us to an area outside the main bath house area.

The bath house was found by Dr Gerald Bodribb, an amateur archaeologist. Guy de la Bédoyère, our Roman expert whose book

Roman Villas and the Countryside had proved invaluable on the live shoot at Turkdean in Gloucestershire in 1997, had contacted us about the site. One of the key ideas he wanted to test was the theory that the bath house did not stand alone and that there would be other buildings such as houses occupied by officers. These officers would have been in charge of the ironworks which would have produced the iron slag under which the bath house had been buried, and it would have been built for them. As Guy said in his initial research document, Britain's natural resources – such as iron – were the property of the Roman emperor and their care would therefore have been the responsibility of high-ranking officials. At an early stage I had wondered whether the baths could have been the equivalent of pithead showers in a coalfield, but he was adamant that only senior officers would have used them, and that most workers would have been little better than slaves.

Guy alerted us to the fact that in Roman times the coastline would have been closer to Beauport Park than it is now, which would have made exporting the finished iron easier than it seems today. This partly helps to explain the anomaly that the bath house is miles from any Roman town or fort.

He also supplied details about the possible name of an officer connected with the bath house. Guy pointed out that an altar at the Roman-Saxon shore fort of Lympne in Kent had been erected by a commander of the fleet, Lucius Aufidius Pantera. By a bit of clever research into other fleet commanders connected with him, Guy had chanced upon Quintus Baienus Blassianus whose name bears a striking similarity to the one recorded on an inscription found at the ironworks: Bassianus. This is the kind of information that unfortunately never makes it into the final programme but is nevertheless fascinating. By and large, *Time Team* is about the results of an excavation – it is not a history programme – but we give the general historical background to set a site in its context.

Henry Cleere, an ex-director of the Council for British Archaeology and one of the experts who worked on the site, believed that the ironworks might be one of the biggest in the Roman Empire. He estimated that it could have yielded more than 200 tons of iron each year – as much as forty per cent of the total produced in Britain. This would have required fifty tons of charcoal a day, destroying massive numbers of hardwood trees in the locality. The large areas of deciduous woodland, including hardwoods like oak, that surround the site today are just a reminder of the vast forests that once covered the region.

In order to understand exactly the nature of what we would be looking for, an understanding of how iron was made would be important. Iron production was in many ways the final stage of a series of metallurgical developments that started with copper and bronze and enabled cultures to use the natural resources that were available to them. Although iron is more common than copper it is harder to extract because it requires a higher temperature. By the Roman period there was a vast requirement for iron which was used for weapons, domestic tools, buildings (nails and cramps) and the whole range of fittings that held boats together.

Iron had not always been acquired by smelting: earlier cultures and native American and Inuit tribes obtained it from meteorites and saw it as a metal from heaven. However, in many areas it is combined with oxygen as an oxide. Magnetite, limonite and haematite are the main forms, some of which can be used as red dyes. Combined with other minerals as ores they require temperatures somewhere in the region of 1,300°C (2,372°F) and the presence of carbon for the iron to be extracted. The ore is mixed with charcoal and as the temperature in the furnace rises the oxygen and other impurities separate out from the ore to form slag. The iron, still with some other materials, forms a bloom at the base of the furnace. This is removed and hammered by a smith to extract the remaining impurities. Slag looks metallic but is largely made of a non-magnetic substance called fairlight. This is one of the main by-products of an ironworks and was useful for building roads because it is easily compacted and drains well.

Iron was used in the Middle East as early as 3,000 BC but in central Europe ironworking is associated with the Hallstatt period of the Early Iron Age (c.800–c.500 BC) and the earliest known examples of iron-smelting furnaces come from Austria at the end of that era. Once the technological problems of extracting iron from ore had been solved it became more easily available and many cultures were able to take advantage of it. Some historians refer to iron as the 'democratic' metal. As smiths began to learn the secrets of the new material, they found that welding sheets of iron that had different degrees of hardness could produce a durable sharp edge. Because iron is worked in the presence of carbon it begins to absorb it and this starts the process that creates the harder metal we call steel.

Dr Gerald Bodribb has spent a large part of his life uncovering the secrets of the site he discovered and it was clear that anything we could

do to support him would be worthwhile. When we first saw the bath house it was in a state of suspended archaeological animation. The walls were protected with plastic bags and the site was covered by a tin roof.

We had come across a bath house, or at least the remains of a plunge pool, at Turkdean. I had by now become cautious about the chances of finding a mosaic. At Turkdean we had uncovered a large villa but no mosaic.

Throughout Britain there are Roman sites of great importance that now lie hidden under sand, which is the standard way of backfilling and protecting excavated buildings. The Beauport Park bath house is in many ways an illustration of why this happens, and why English Heritage and other archaeological bodies are so cautious about uncovering additional sites. The reasons are fairly clear. Inevitably, they can begin to deteriorate when they are uncovered. Weather and the attention of vandals can soon begin to damage unique archaeology and the bill to stabilize and protect a site can be huge. It would be almost

Above: Beneath the tin sheets and sand the standing walls of a Roman bath house survived.

Team Profile

Katy Hirst – *Digger*

'My first practical experience of archaeology was at the age of eighteen when my father, who was working in the Middle East, managed to get me on to a site in Oman that was being excavated by Italian archaeologists. I went on to do a degree in archaeology at Durham University and have been a professional archaeologist since 1992. My most exciting find was a Bronze Age necklace with a gold pendant that I found on a child skeleton in Syria. The period I most enjoy studying is prehistory, in particular the rituals.

'The job can be quite strenuous, particularly on *Time Team* when you need to complete a lot of work in a short space of time, which piles on the pressure. I first worked on the series when they were looking for diggers while on a shoot in Carlisle. They contacted the Carlisle unit where I work and I leapt at the opportunity, much to the envy of my fellow archaeologists. Of the *Time Team* digs I have been on, I particularly enjoyed the Roman site at Papcastle because of the rich source of finds that we uncovered.

'I would urge anyone considering archaeology as a career to think very carefully, because it is not a profession that will make you rich. If it seems desirable despite this, I would suggest taking a university course because it is very difficult to get into it through straight digging. For myself, the process of uncovering something amazing that has been hidden for hundreds, even thousands, of years is tremendously rewarding.'

impossible to meet the projected cost without a favourable lottery bid. The English Heritage's response to knowing about an important but buried Roman site is often that it is best to leave it until they can find some way of protecting it and meeting the bill for its care. One of the largest mosaics in southern Britain is buried in Woodchester in Wiltshire, but it will probably never be seen by our generation because

Above: *Gerald Bodribb, who found the bath house, looks on as a local archaeologist shows Phil and Carenza records from the previous digs.*

there are no funds to display and protect it. The irony is, of course, that until a site is exposed it is impossible to tell what condition it is in, and therefore whether it is worth pursuing and what the likely costs will be.

Gerald had gathered a group of enthusiastic helpers around him, some of whom claimed that they could use divining rods to locate archaeology. They had toiled around the bath-house site attempting to trace other areas of Roman activity. Without any funds their work had always been voluntary. They were dependent on their own devices and without the benefit of advice from professional architects had often not recorded opened-up areas and small trial digs accurately. In some cases it seemed that digs had been cut through the archaeology in order to pursue a particular find.

Inevitably, there was a lack of adequate plans and careful mapping of finds, and no section drawings showing the sides of trenches and recording the various layers and where finds were located. Any archaeological judgement of Beauport Park would be hampered

Above: Showing considerable job
flexibility our researchers turn
into forest clearance experts in
the search for Roman buildings.

because in many cases all we knew was that Roman pottery and other artefacts had come from various holes scattered throughout the site. There was plenty of evidence of activity, but without consistent records of the exact distribution, location, depth and quality of the material it was difficult to decide where the key areas were located.

On the first day I was given a guided tour of the site, particularly the area hidden under the woods bordering the small stream that runs through it. As we staggered through the nettles and waist-high weeds various diggings were pointed out to me. There seemed to be rather a lot of them and as the cartoon shows it reminded us of gruyère cheese.

Guy and Gerald had discussed possible targets in the areas surrounding the site with us. An initial survey by Gerald and his team had located platforms that might be the possible site of buildings, and these were the areas we decided to concentrate on initially. They would be the location for our first three trenches. They were about 110 metres (366 feet) from the bath house and each one was just large enough –

about ninety square metres (270 square feet) – to encompass a building. There were two obstacles to excavating them: thick undergrowth and the fact that the site was surrounded by the green fairways of the golf course. The first day's events took on a rather surreal quality as we excavated alongside the golfers' paths with the odd ball sailing over our heads.

Each site required a major effort to clear the bracken and brushwood so that the geophysics team could do its survey. The initial results were disappointing and as we began to cast our net further afield I looked again at the bath house site, and wondered whether we should be dealing with a much smaller area immediately to its north-west. A large area here had been scheduled but within it there were open excavations that had not, as far as we could tell, been drawn or recorded. At this stage I thought it might be useful if we recorded them. However, we first had to obtain permission to work in the scheduled area.

The local English Heritage inspector, Peter Kendall, took the view that recording the existing excavations more accurately and providing drawings of the section would be a valuable piece of work in terms of understanding the site, and sanctioned a limited exercise to record it. I agreed with him that before we proceeded we would check with Andy Woodcock, the county archaeologist, who had agreed to act as our archaeological policeman. He proved to be a tremendous help.

Jenni Butterworth was sent into the woods to record the open digs and first had to clear the vegetation. Only one small excavation within the scheduled area could be easily accessed, where Roman pottery had been located but no section drawings had been done.

By the end of Day One we had drawn a blank with the first platform site even though we had put three trenches in there, and had to expand our area. Jenni had had some success in extracting slag from the hole left by a fallen tree which we were calling Trench 4. But we still didn't have any buildings. We were working on the idea that the high ground surrounding the ironworkings was a likely location for a villa. Mick and I strolled away from the excavation and filming in order to explore some of these areas.

fact that a particular line of bricks in Trench 2 was the most likely location of the key archaeology, which enabled him to put more filming time into that area. At Beauport Park I felt that the high ground around the site might prove unproductive and suggested concentrating on the area in the vicinity of the bath house. We had by now put Trenches 5 and 6 into earthworks that Stewart felt might indicate buildings but had located little initial evidence.

I need to know what the potential problems are and the likely route of the archaeology because once a director is caught up in the immediacy of working out how to shoot a scene and putting sequences together, he or she will not be aware of the undercurrents. These only become apparent through looking closely at the trenches and listening carefully to what Phil and the main excavators have to say. The big advantage of using our own diggers, even as part of a larger local team, is that over the years they have become aware of the needs of the programme, and understand that if they find something that might be critical to the story I need to know about it as soon as possible.

At Beauport Park there was always the 'subtext' that work had already been done, and that it was difficult to interpret it because of the

Below: Mick playing with his favourite toy – a helicopter, frequently used for aerial shots. The pilot is under strict instructions not to be dragged away for a visit to all the local ecclesiastical sites.

Behind the Scenes at *Time Team*

absence of standard archaeological records. This potentially created tension between the various teams working on the site, and was typical of the kind of undercurrent I need to spot – it might become part of the story, or prevent the excavation running smoothly.

Tony and I have always had an understanding of the need to exchange information about the subtext. We are on the lookout for the reality that the archaeologists are not telling us about – some event that is hidden by the frenetic activity in the trenches. This often involves human dramas played out behind the scenes. During an excavation at St Mary's City in Maryland in the United States we had discussed the fact that there was an obvious cultural difference between how we carried out our digging and the American way of excavating. This discussion led to Tony's PTC acknowledging the difference. His role as both presenter and associate producer means that he can contribute in a general way to the route the programme is taking and alert us if anything goes awry from his point of view.

Above: *Phil and local archaeologists scrape at the edge of the thirteenth fairway looking for signs of iron-smelting activity.*

Above: *The complications of a trench dug at different levels at different times without standardizing recording procedure. Carenza tries to make sense of it.*

In the case of Beauport Park it was Tony who first suggested to Graham Dixon, the director, that the opening PTC should have a more general goal than had been stated in the script because it seemed likely that we should not nail our colours too firmly to the mast of finding buildings other than the bath house. It is interesting to see the difference between the shooting script and what Tony actually said on screen.

Before:
'But a Roman bath house wouldn't have been built on its own, forty miles from the nearest Roman town. What were the Romans doing here miles away from any other Roman buildings, buried here just waiting to be found? *Time Team* have just three days to investigate!'

After:
'But what is a Roman bath house doing here completely on its own forty miles from the nearest Roman town? What was happening around here 1,900 years ago? *Time Team* have just three days to find out!'

The walk in the woods with Mick yielded one potential earthwork site, which we were going to call Trench 7 – this was found to be the remnants of old quarrying activity – and the outline of a strategy that would lead us to attempt to examine all the areas of high ground around it. We were not confident or hopeful of success. The woodland did not feel as though Roman structures were concealed beneath it, but we had a plan and we would try to pursue it logically. This meant there would be an early start on Day Two and that our diggers and two researchers, Jules and David, would turn into a forest clearance crew.

Day Two saw us pursuing the hunt for buildings. The excavations in Trench 5 and Trench 6 showed little evidence of occupation by the middle of the day and we began to think we might be dealing with a site that was concentrated around the bath house. Villas or other structures might exist further away. Possibly the Roman overseers, like us, would have wanted to live a good distance away from their work. However, Guy insisted that the bath house should not be just standing on its own; there should be other buildings because that was the typical pattern. We

Below: Stewart Ainsworth conducts a review of our strategy based on his survey of the wider landscape.

Following Page: Where are we going? Graham Dixon and Tony contemplate the changes we may need to make if the archaeology proves elusive, and how these are best explained to the viewer.

than the experts had predicted. I was surprised at how small it was: I had imagined a large structure but this looked like an oversized beehive. Once it was dry, ore and locally produced charcoal were fed into it and a team of helpers manned bellows to keep the fire going. Gerry checked the heat level in the furnace with a temperature gauge, and at a critical point the furnace was closed off, reduction took place and the slag was tapped off.

Waiting for it to appear was an anxious time – and even when the volcanic-like substance dripped from the furnace we weren't sure whether there was anything left in the kiln. If there had been too many impurities in the ore there would be huge amounts of slag and no bloom. All went well, however, and the final act of extracting the iron and working it in raw form was a fascinating piece of reconstruction. To see material that had a day earlier been rock-like ore turned into a metal that glinted in the sun was a major *Time Team* achievement.

As we watched our group of reconstruction experts toiling in the heat we had some idea, for the first time, of what the site might have looked like during the Roman period. There would have been hundreds of these furnaces, and thousands of smiths working the hot iron into shape.

Opposite: Jake Keen charging the furnace with ore and charcoal, a critical stage in the making of iron.

Above: A crucial moment. Tapping the slag tells us if the furnace has done its work. The crew braved the heat and smoke to get the best position to film Phil and Jake's spontaneous reaction.

Following page: The glowing evidence of success. Phil holds the spongy bit of iron that would become the end product of our three days' labour.

Team Profile

Ella Galinski– *Associate Producer*

'I have been with *Time Team* since the beginning of the series and worked as assistant producer on the preceding *Time Signs* programmes, which was when I first became interested in archaeology.

'After gaining an MA in Drama and Theatre Arts, I moved into acting and, amongst other things, toured Europe with the Fragile Theatre Company, which was based in Italy. Later, having damaged my voice, I decided to concentrate on production and, after a brief spell as a set designer for an advertizing photographer, I joined Videotext who, at that time, were making educational videos. As in any small company I did everything from making sandwiches to writing, shooting and editing my own material.

'*Time Team* is such a people orientated production and I love trying to capture the spontaneous emotions on screen – the enthusiasm, excitement and disappointment as the narrative unfolds.

'The iron smelting experiment at Beauport Park was one of the most difficult and satisfying challenges. The atmosphere amongst the group of enthusiasts attempting the almost impossible within three days was quite electric and when the alchemy occurred the sense of achievement was thrilling. These cameos are often logistically tricky because you can rarely stop the action and shoot again – you have to capture everything as it happens. However, this makes for good television as it captures all the excitement as it evolves.'

Opposite: Hammering out the final piece of iron sent sparks flying and reproduced a skill that had last taken place on this site 1,700 years ago.

The lack of any buildings meant that we were now concentrating on evidence of ironworking. We had begun to get better geophysics results from areas nearer the main fairway. An earlier excavation had located a furnace and it seemed that Trench 9, the trench Jenni was clearing up, also contained the fired base of one. Each trench brought us nearer the edge of the golf course and we had to rely on the goodwill of

the owners to allow us to dig closer to the fairway – and the speed of the diggers' reactions to evade the golf balls. Trench 10 went into the edge of the rough on the thirteenth fairway.

On Day Three, Carenza and Phil spent some time working alongside members of the local group in Trench 11, an area that had been excavated previously. They were able to show the local archaeologists a standardized set of digging and recording methods that archaeologists use to understand the site. Trenches 12 and 13 followed on more earthworks. Our efforts began to have all the appearance of what my father calls a 'poke and hope' strategy, until Trench 13 found a furnace base and Trench 14, our last big geophysics target, located a charcoal-working pit. Charcoal is a key ingredient of ironworking because it allows a higher temperature to be reached in the furnace and there would have been a number of charcoal-burning sites in the area around the ironworks.

Below: *With a quick rub from a file, Phil is able to catch the sunlight glinting on the surface of the finished product.*

Conclusion

It now looks as if the fleet officers who managed the ironworks lived some distance away, perhaps by the coast, and only made passing visits to the site. There is a chance, however, that their accommodation lies under the piles of slag that surround the bath house. In the words of Guy de la Bédoyère, the programme showed that 'in practice the Roman world wasn't always quite as predictable as is sometimes thought… nothing in archaeology is certain, but theories need to be formed and tested for there to be any progress'. The lack of mosaics in the bath house possibly hinted at a low-status establishment suitable for the use of local workers.

Beauport Park is typical of many archaeological sites which would have remained undiscovered without the enthusiastic hard work of amateur archaeologists such as the ones on the *Time Team* dig and it is clear that groups like these need help. With county archaeology departments strapped for cash and manpower, and under pressure to dig up a site for a bypass or supermarket, it is often difficult to support them. When a site is as potentially important as Beauport Park the all too likely response is to stop any further work, schedule it to give it some legal protection and then cover it. Resources for archaeology are finite, and bodies such as English Heritage have to decide which sites should receive their limited cash and which ones will have to be left fallow.

Above: *After a tiring weekend the final piece of business needs to be thrashed out. What can Tony say we have achieved? Director Graham Dixon and I work out the possibilities. Tony will then turn this into his own style for the camera.*

Following page: *Despite the archaeological frustrations of the site, the success of the ironworking and intensive team effort gave us all a feeling of pleasure at the end of the three days.*

CHAPTER 4

Smallhythe, Kent

TONY'S PIECE TO CAMERA: 'You wouldn't think that these ordinary looking fields and this marshy old drainage ditch had anything to do with Britain's great sea-going heritage – for a start, I'm miles from the coast at a place called Smallhythe in Kent. But around the time of the battle of Agincourt in the early 1400s, somewhere round here was a port and a royal shipyard big enough to build 1,000-ton battleships. But if that's true, where are they now? And where's the river or estuary where they launched great big wooden ships?'

Opposite: This large trench with relatively few finds did eventually produce evidence of the silting that caused Smallhythe's demise.

Above: A 'delft' field. We would, by the end of Day Two, have placed a considerable number of trenches in this field.

Medieval Shipbuilding

There is an enigma about medieval shipbuilding. We have good documentary records of the names of ships, the kings they were built for and, in some cases, paintings of these huge vessels with their flags proudly flying. Thanks to the excavation of wrecks like the *Mary Rose*, we also know what they would have contained. However, we know very little about the medieval dockyards in which they were built.

In the Middle Ages ships were among the primary weapons of war, built to carry battle into foreign realms. In times of peace they were often neglected and allowed to rot. This meant that the shipbuilding industry was always a source of irregular employment that was dependent on the whim of the king.

Smallhythe was at that time a port and the surrounding area, especially the Weald, would have provided the basic requirements for shipbuilding – iron ore for iron and woodland for timber. The 1,000 ton *Jesus* was built here, or nearby, in 1416 during the reign of Henry V (1413–22). He was also responsible for the 1,400 ton *Grace Dieu*. Remnants of this great ship still survive. Built in Southampton it was part of the fleet that carried Henry's army to France in the campaign that ended victoriously with the battle of Agincourt in 1415.

Henry VII (1485–1509) increased the British fleet with ships like the *Sovereign*

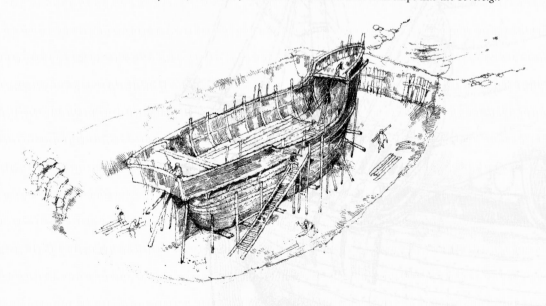

and the 1,000-ton *Regent*. The *Mary Fortune*, an eighty-oared barque, was built at Smallhythe in 1497. Ian Friel our medieval ship expert was able to tell us details about the *Mary Fortune*. Work began on 11 February and went on for sixteen weeks. The total cost of wages and material amounted to over £110 – more than nine years' wages for the skilled master shipwright in charge of the work. There were at least sixteen other shipwrights as well as sawyers, eight sailmakers, some labourers and a night-watchman. The ship consumed at least twenty-three tons of timber and more than 13,000 iron and wooden nails, along with many other items. The *Mary Fortune*'s five sails were sewn with 112 'sail needles' and the three-masted rig required eighty separate ropes. The basic timber and iron raw material probably all came from within a few miles of Smallhythe.

We believed that the edge of the Rother river which flowed past Smallhythe in the Middle Ages would have been an ideal site for a shipyard. However, on the first day of filming, as we stared at the flat landscape sixteen kilometres (ten miles) from the sea it was difficult to imagine magnificent boats being built here.

A recurring theme and regularly stated aim of many *Time Team* programmes is to get what Mick calls 'the bigger picture'. This effectively means putting the dig into its historical context and usually involves understanding the wider landscape around the site. My more cynical side suspects that even if the Ark of Covenant turned up in a Yorkshire valley Mick would still be trying to put it into its context for the first few days: 'OK, so it's the Ark of the Covenant, but what were the local mining community up to in the recent past and how do these slag heaps fit into the picture?'

On an archaeological site it is often a mistake to get too focused on a single idea or target as this frequently means that you miss elements of the context that might hold critical clues to the question you are asking. This is what happened at Smallhythe. In the Middle Ages the village was on the Rother river which was wide and deep enough to be easily navigated. We knew that ships had been built there. We also knew that it had been important enough for Henry V to visit it in the early fifteenth century. Today the remains of what was once a thriving port and the community that built the *Jesus*, one of the biggest ships in his navy, have disappeared under farmland and the sea is sixteen kilometres (ten miles) distant.

The site was suggested to us by Christine O'Neill, the town clerk for Tenterden in Kent, and we had some clues to the location of a dockyard. A field near the site was called the delft field and the word 'delft' implies diggings. Could an enclosed dockyard be buried underneath it? If such a dock did exist we might have to deal with deep deposits and fragile wooden structures at their edges. Brian Philip, the local archaeologist, was keen to dig deep into the area with a mechanical digger but this might not be the best strategy on a site of this importance.

If the enclosed dockyard was our focus there were two larger issues to bear in mind. First, not all big ships were built in enclosed dockyards. Gustav Milne, our archaeological expert on the subject, and Mick gave two examples: Poole in Dorset and Buckler's Hard in Hampshire, where there is evidence that large boats had been built on beaches. Second, occupation in the area may well have been seasonal and therefore little evidence would be left. The key context that might be helpful was where the channel of the Rother had been in the fifteenth century. This might provide a limit to the site and an approximate location for shipbuilding. We hoped that our geophysics team and Sue Ovenden, who was in charge of the seismics, could find the different levels of infill and map the early shape of the estuary.

On Day One we pursued the 'delft' site and Stewart ranged over the wider area looking for lumps and bumps. There were basically two possibilities: the ships were built either in docks or in slips or depressions cut into the beach. The delft field yielded little except large piles of sediment and clay, and black deposits. Gustav Milne thought the deposits might be prehistoric and managed to extract large pieces of wood from them. But there were no artefacts and no ships' nails, the most common find on a shipbuilding site. By the end of the day, six trenches had been dug in the field labelled 1a to 1f.

While Sue got on with the seismics, John and Chris located some hot spots, areas of high magnetic activity that might indicate occupation or even industrial processes. By the end of Day One we had found pieces of farmyard rubbish and a drain cover, but no signs of shipbuilding activity. As Chris commented, it was more Ford Cortina than foundry.

Originally the port house, Smallhythe Place is a late-fifteenth century building and the National Trust, which owns it, had told us that ships' nails had been found in the pond at its back. The aerial photograph showed a larger area of water that could possibly have been a dock. Carenza's job was to follow this line of enquiry and, having been sent packing from the Trust's nice garden – 'No you can't put a trench in here' – had gone into the fields next door where there was a pond in a similar alignment, and where Gustav suggested shipbuilding slips may have been. Would the pond's mud hold any more clues?

Following page: The first sniff of decent archaeology. Phil points out the key bits while Ian Powesland, in the foreground, stands by with the mini-digger to remove more topsoil. The plastic under the spoil is to protect the grass.

By Day Two we had little to show archaeologically for our efforts and John and Chris widened their search. However, we had started on the cameo, which was to become a really positive element in the programme. If you can't find a boat why not build one? The idea was to make a section of a ship from timber held together with iron nails and roves – the diamond-shaped washers that are placed over the ends of nails. This would be done by Andrew Baldwin, a smith, and Damian Goodburn who was a veteran of many *Time Team* reconstructions.

Damian and a team of carpenters had made a prehistoric log boat at Llangorse in Powys in Series 1 and the A-frame section of a medieval house for the Plympton, Devon, programme in Series 6. Even his best friends would admit that he is something of a slave-driver and a total perfectionist when he is engaged in his trade. He spares no one in his pursuit of the perfect wooden construction and regards the sappy green wood of freshly felled oak with almost religious fervour.

I have fond memories of the beautiful surface of the Llangorse boat, the wood newly felled and cut with a traditional adze. Constructing it had one of the essential requirements of a cameo: it was almost impossible to achieve. When we first contacted Damian about

Opposite: John Gater giving the archaeology a good belt. The hammer blow creates the necessary vibration to begin recording seismic responses.

Above: Jane Siddell and Keith Wilkinson checking core samples. This gradually accumulated enough evidence to draw a profile of the area.

Team Profile

Peter Bellamy – *Excavation Report Writer*

'When I was about eight years old I was introduced to an archaeological dig just up the road from where I lived. The diggers gave me a few pieces of Bronze Age pottery – nothing terribly special, but they were very important to me at the time and I still have them. Ever since then I had a yearning to make archaeology my career.

'I have been an archaeologist since 1976 and my favourite eras would have to be the Neolithic and Bronze Age periods because I like flint objects and enjoy the challenge of prehistory. I get very excited when I discover scatters of flint on the surface of fields because it generally gives you clues as to whether there was a prehistoric settlement there.

'The most time-consuming part of my job on *Time Team* is writing up sites after the digs. I am very concerned about keeping a proper archaeological record, including sketches and photographs, of everything we find in the trenches. Sorting through a pile of records on my own, putting them in order and making sure the site is finished after everyone else is long gone is probably the hardest, not to mention loneliest, part of my job.

'When I mention my involvement with the programme to my colleagues most of them are impressed and interested, while some consider it hard work. I would advise anyone contemplating a career as an archaeologist to go on a few digs before they decide, and perhaps try and do something allied to it – geology or conservation, for example. Archaeology is not well paid and there are few job prospects, but if you are the right person it is a wonderful thing to do. For me personally the chance to use my muscles and my head at the same time is very rewarding.'

Damian used a mixture of wool and tar to waterproof the planks – but just how to combine them was a problem. Was the wool dipped in the tar first? Or was the tar applied and the wool stuck on to it? We tried both methods. Dipping was expensive and wasted too much expensive tar, so we applied the tar first and then the wool, which gradually absorbed the tar.

A sketch of the structure was a useful prop and allowed viewers to see how small sections might have been assembled into a boat in the fourteenth and fifteenth centuries.

By the middle of Day Two John and Chris's extended search paid off and we found some archaeology at last: the remains of a slipway, a large area of brick rubble that may have been a kiln, a slip next to it and, finally, some ships' nails.

Stewart's search for lumps and bumps in the fields provided the first hint that there was a string of depressions that were possibly the surfaces of slips, and an aerial map showed a series of similar features. Could these be shipbuilding sites? We dug a new trench, Trench 4, towards the area of the medieval river channel and this produced a large area of sand. Although not exactly gripping from a visual point of view, it confirmed that sand had built up slowly at the water's edge. Large numbers of laminations or layers were visible in the section. It was these deposits that had finished the site off as a port. Run-off from land

Above: Getting in close to Damian Goodburn and Phil working on the cameo.

Above: Phil concentrates on the final stages of the cameo.

reclaimed by farmers gradually silted up the river and prevented the tides from clearing the estuary. The result was that by the early seventeenth century only small ships could reach Smallhythe.

Ships require metalwork, tar and bricks – each of the galleons would have had a brick fire-box – and one of our main goals was to see if there were any traces in the area of the industries involved in providing these. Dana Goodburn Brown, a metallurgist and Damian's partner, was happy to provide an answer. We set her to work around two sites – Trench 5, which Phil was digging and which had revealed more of a brick structure, and Trenches 6 and 7 which had been newly opened in the

fields behind Smallhythe Place. Dana's speciality is historical metalworking and she began by searching through piles of soil with a magnet. She was looking for two types of material: the splinters that break off heated metal when it is hammered on an anvil, and the metallic balls that are first seen as sparks when a red-hot bar of metal is hammered. The soil was damp and she had to dry it out first, which produced the rather strange sight of an archaeologist drying a spoil heap with a hairdryer.

Once collected, the small fragments were examined under a microscope and compared with material from the smithing we were doing back at the incident room. There was an exact match with the fragments from the trench behind Smallhythe Place. Once again this shows the advantage of skilled workers reproducing historical activities on site. The metal Dana had discovered proved that metalworking had taken place on the site.

The relative lack of activity in the delft area gave me a chance to enjoy one of my favourite *Time Team* activities: sitting on the side of Phil's trench. His forensic skill with his trowel is based on years of experience and over the several years I have watched him I have learned invaluable lessons in how archaeologists work, and why they dig a trench in a particular way. Just listening to Phil talk through the reality of the kinds of material he is digging gives an idea of how his perception works. There was a variation in the soil around the brick structure in the main trench. Phil commented: 'You can see that the dirt is a different colour from the dirt outside the brick area – it's darker and as you tap it, it feels solid like it was built in place.' His initial perception changes as he begins to work out the logic of the trench from the different textures and densities of the material in front of him.

I have learnt from listening to this kind of dialogue that the process of understanding a trench takes time, and that the archaeology needs to be analysed layer by layer. Each one provides a context and the finds in that context may help to date the layer. If an excavator is certain that a layer lies completely over the top of a section, it may suggest that it is later than the section. This can be critical to trying to understand the archaeology.

Archaeologists always avoid plucking a find from a layer or context because it could have its origins in a lower layer and this may be the only thing that dates the layer above it. Another concern, often expressed by excavators on *Time Team*, is the need to avoid treading on a surface that has been cleaned – the final stage in revealing a layer or context. This is the moment when subtle differences may appear in the surface and need to be recorded. Recording can mean drawing a complete and detailed view of the trench and I have to be patient while this is done. Watching a digger carefully draw bits of brick or pot and record them on a gridded surface requires Zen-like patience. It is not a

Below: Tony keeps the viewers informed with another key PTC. Nick Dance captures the moment.

gripping process from the point of view of the director – in this case Alex West – but it has to be done. Until the archaeological recording is complete we cannot go into a deeper layer.

It can take hours of hard work to complete this final stage and Tony and the crew have learned to always ask the diggers' permission before treading in a trench. Once cleared, the layer can be photographed and if necessary we move on to the next one. It is an interesting moment when a layer that Phil has been protecting like a doting mother is removed to see what lies beneath it.

At Smallhythe the key finds we were searching for were ships' nails and these gradually began to emerge from the edge of Phil's Trench 5. Some appeared to be unused and others were badly corroded. Carenza had begun to clear out the pond in the fields adjoining Smallhythe Place but the material that came from it contained modern debris and lacked nails. It looked as though another

potential dockyard site had been knocked on the head. However, we now had geophysics data from this area and there were some hot spots (the site of Trench 6). Mick Worthington joined Carenza to investigate these and their initial investigations produced a kettle. More work would be needed on Day Three.

On the second night of the dig there was an interesting *Time Team* moment: 'the turnaround'. At the end of a long day, although everyone has stopped working and concentrating on the site, conversations continue and people get the chance to exchange views and ideas.

A conclave of experts gathered in the bar of the Ashford International Hotel and a new idea emerged. Gustav Milne had been reflecting on the wood we had found in the delft trenches. What if it wasn't prehistoric? Maybe it was more recent. Had boats been beached rather than built in the area where we been digging? Might boats have been dismantled there? Had it been a backwater wreckers' yard? If a shallow bay had existed at

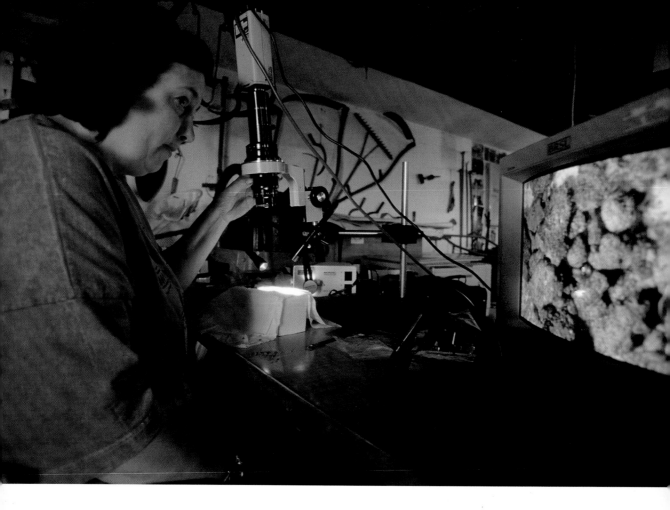

the edges of the delft field this might provide an answer to these questions. We would have to return to the dig and see. The obvious solution – getting the wood carbon-dated – was just not available within *Time Team*'s three days.

On Day Three, to determine whether a bay existed, we ran a line of core samples up to the edge of the delft field to see if, for example, they showed the profile of an inlet. They didn't, and instead showed a gradually shelving beach which would have been too shallow to accommodate large vessels. Although it couldn't have been for shipbuilding, the exercise was very important in defining the limits of shipbuilding activity. However, we did make further progress in Carenza's field and Trench 6. She began to find a line of ships' nails within the outline of a boat-shaped depression below the kettle. Mick Aston was a little sceptical, but further work and Carenza's explanation – she can be very persuasive – finally convinced him. As we excavated deeper, the shape that held the nails took on the appearance of a small boat that had perhaps been used to reinforce the river bank.

Trench 6 had a sequel. It is amazing how often a final piece of evidence appears the day after a *Time Team* shoot, when the cameras have gone and the trenches are being finally recorded and backfilled. In this case we found a section of boat similar to the one Damian had constructed. We are in a dilemma when this happens. The temptation is to include the find in some kind of postscript, but by and large we don't do this. *Time Team* keeps to its three-day structure. On one occasion – a programme at Launceston, Cornwall – we gave the carbon-14 dating for a skeleton we had found on the site of a leper colony because it was critical to our interpretation of the site, but this is a rare example.

The slipway in Phil's Trench 5 also provided a satisfactory conclusion, while the brickwork turned out to be a kiln, possibly used to fire bricks, and part of a small industrial area alongside the shipbuilding site.

Although Smallhythe had many enjoyable elements it left me feeling slightly dissatisfied. In retrospect, it felt like a programme that we got strategically wrong. It exposed the problems of doing archaeology in three days. It is difficult to sort a site out if your initial hypothesis – in this case our focus on an enclosed dockyard – is

Below: *Even after a long day the chat still keeps going. Brendan Hughes, the second unit director, talks through ideas with Alex West, Mick Worthington and assistant producer Tory Batten.*

Above: *Phil applying the forensic trowel. The bucket in the foreground contains his 'loose'.*

Opposite: *Victor's cartoon shows Robin Bush who was keen to sample the products of a local vineyard.*

incorrect. On reflection I would have liked to have given Stewart more time to look at the lumps and bumps and to have looked at the wider picture at an earlier stage. More time would have also allowed John to investigate what was once Smallhythe's main road. The need for geophysics to operate more widely than normal meant that some areas had to be missed out, and the hunt for the so-called dockyard took our attention away from ones that might have been more profitable. It would have been great to dig the settlement area but we ran out of time.

Pursuing the 'clue' of the delft site and its shape was logical. Local historians and writers, and our own research, had suggested that this was the best place to start our search for the shipbuilding site but we had spent a whole day and dug six trenches with no return. I also feel that the local view that the ponds behind Smallhythe Place could have been a harbour sidetracked us. This clearly turned out not to be the case. As Mick says, we told future archaeologists where the shipbuilding sites weren't – but it was obviously frustrating from a programme point of view.

A plus was the data we had collected on the original channel of the Rother. Jane with her 'coring' and Sue with her seismics did a fantastic job of showing its depths and size. We used seismics twice in this series, in Cooper's Hole as well as at Smallhythe, and it came up with very valuable data on both occasions – much to everybody's surprise because the initial action of smacking a hammer into the ground or exploding a shell seems a little Heath Robinson – and we hope to use it again in future. Jane's work with coring showed that an entirely different approach that complemented the sesmics could produce the same set of answers and gave us excellent, solid evidence of the different layers of the original river channel. This is valuable work that will enable future archaeologists to understand the site better.

Conclusion

Although we left Smallhythe with something of an air of disappointment, feeling that we had not achieved all that we might have done, two months later Gustav's research painted a very different picture. He had taken all our finds and the report of what we had uncovered to the Institute of Archaeology at University College London

Following page: *Carenza poking through the debris from the pond site. Joe Ellison, when not metal detecting, is responsible for communications, enabling all of us to talk to each other.*

CHAPTER 5

Reedham Marshes, Norfolk

TONY'S PIECE TO CAMERA: 'Just over fifty years ago, this tranquil Norfolk fenland was the scene of a tragic, and unsolved, wartime mystery. It was February 1944, and in the sky above 300 American bombers were returning from a mission over Germany. Minutes away from the safety of base, one of the bombers suddenly collided with another and the two aircraft plummeted to earth somewhere here in Reedham Marshes. All twenty-one crew were killed. So what happened? ... We'll be excavating one of the planes, in the hope its carcass may yield some clues; and we'll be trying to find out as much as we can about the two crews, and the sequence of events that led to the crash.'

Opposite: Start them young – a junior helper gets stuck in to a spoil heap at the edge of the site.

Above: The opening night and a lot of experts have come to spread their accumulated wisdom.

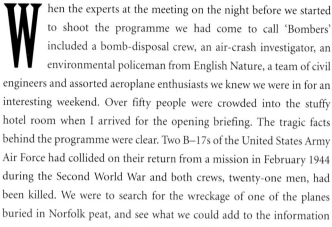

When the experts at the meeting on the night before we started to shoot the programme we had come to call 'Bombers' included a bomb-disposal crew, an air-crash investigator, an environmental policeman from English Nature, a team of civil engineers and assorted aeroplane enthusiasts we knew we were in for an interesting weekend. Over fifty people were crowded into the stuffy hotel room when I arrived for the opening briefing. The tragic facts behind the programme were clear. Two B–17s of the United States Army Air Force had collided on their return from a mission in February 1944 during the Second World War and both crews, twenty-one men, had been killed. We were to search for the wreckage of one of the planes buried in Norfolk peat, and see what we could add to the information about the causes of the crash.

At the front of the room the flight sergeant from bomb disposal was well into his stride describing the lethal potential of a Browning 0.50 inch machine-gun round with a clarity that drew the blood from Carenza's face and had Phil making a strange sound that I have come to recognize over the years – something between a hysterical giggle and a long-drawn-out 'Errr...' The fact that over 6,000 of these rounds might be scattered around the crash site concentrated everyone's attention.

Work on 'Bombers' had begun to get complicated two months earlier. A series of events was triggered by the somewhat late identification of the area of the crash as a Site of Special Scientific Interest. SSSIs are notified under the Wildlife and Countryside Act 1981, in recognition of their special biological and/or geological interest. Notification has to be given to English Nature before specified activities can be carried out on the sites, in part to reduce the hostility to wildlife of the surrounding land and protect the quality of the water and air environments. Whatever we did in the area would also have to be cleared by the Environment Agency.

Below: *Carenza examined two rounds from a B–17 machine gun. They still have their bullets attached and are potentially 'live'. RAF bomb disposal made them safe shortly afterwards.*

To get clearance to work on a vulnerable and protected site we had to define the size of the trench or trenches we wanted to dig and get the area they would cover surveyed beforehand. Exact dimensions were unclear at this stage because we could not tell precisely where and how the plane had crashed. The bigger the trench, the bigger the bill for the survey. The cost of a survey that would cover every potential excavation area might be so high that it would prevent the programme going ahead at all. It seemed appropriate that on this particular excavation we were facing an element of catch-22.

I had always thought that 'Bombers' would be an exciting programme. It would show archaeology being applied to a new and different subject for *Time Team* and in that sense would be 'educational' for viewers. And we all felt that the potential difficulties would produce a classic *Time Team* struggle against the odds – one of the elements of a more interesting programme – with, hopefully, a successful conclusion. Sites that appear to have a direct and easy route to a predictable outcome do not have the right feel for the series.

Above: *Water from our excavation had to be drained into an artificial pond. Local engineers, Mules Engineering, helped to create the structure to deal with the problems we faced.*

Following page: *Pictures of members of B–17 crews. The site generated masses of ephemera and technical manuals.*

Above: *Running repairs to Mr Harding's second-best shirt by Ms Lewis.*

excavate. No one knows a machine as well as the person who has had to make or maintain it.

The crash investigator would soon be able to make his initial judgements, but by the end of Day One none of the critical pieces of plane had been found and John and Sue's geophysics had produced no sign of a big response that could be the engines.

As Day Two got under way I became increasingly concerned that we hadn't resolved a key problem: the exact location of the main crash and the angle of dive of the plane as it entered the peat. Stewart believed that it had plunged down vertically, probably into the part of the site now occupied by a dyke but nothing appeared when we began to delve into that area with the mechanical digger's longest extension arm. The alternative possibility was that the plane had come in at a shallow angle and belly flopped, travelling along the ground and scattering wreckage far and wide. There were odd ambiguities in some of the remains. Two glass navigation lights remained intact – would these have survived a massive vertical impact?

Back at the 'Bombers' site we were relying on three pieces of information to give us an idea of the crash location: an aerial photograph of what seemed to be the wreckage and showed an area that could be roughly identified because woods that had been there in 1944 still existed; and eyewitness reports and colour photographs from an earlier dig that had located the propeller. Using all three, Stewart and Mick made their best guess as to the epicentre of the crash. However, there was no response when we searched the area with geophysics.

Day Three at last began to produce the significant finds we had hoped for, but the location of the engines and the main fuselage remains a mystery. From Trench 2, our main trench, we had already retrieved fragments of cockpit glass and personal items that brought home the reality of the crash. These included parachute harnesses, a piece of a flying cap, a pilot's boot, a glove and the armed back of the pilot's seat.

We began to use all our geophysics and metal detectors in unison, getting each of them to crosscheck each response. John and his team scanned the surfaces of both trenches and as we got lower in the excavations we asked the RAF team to use their detecting gear to go over the same areas. We followed a significant response in Trench 2 and up

Below: Stewart Ainsworth using the photographs to suggest a possible location for the crash.

Following page: The broad Norfolk landscape with its dykes and fens had preserved the secrets of the crash for fifty years. The dimensions of the main trench would set us a series of major civil-engineering challenges.

Right: Jenni Butterworth cleans a parachute harness, one of the finds that brought us closer to the people who had died.

Opposite: The RAF bomb-disposal crew in action with their detecting gear. Meanwhile Ian McLachlan discusses likely findings.

to five metres (fifteen feet) – well beyond the depth at which I was prepared to risk a human digger – we found first one and then another B–17 machine gun. Once again we were helped by the excellent skills of the digger drivers. This was an astonishing piece of luck. The .50-calibre Brownings were one of the key weapons of defence. They could fire at 760 rounds per minute and were much more effective than the .303 calibre machine guns on fighters such as the Spitfire.

The RAF bomb-disposal team immediately moved into action and, after washing down the guns, discovered a live round in the breech of one of them. This was potentially deadly and care had to be taken to make it safe. Ian Powesland, one of our diggers, probably enjoyed one of his best moments as he got to carry a disarmed gun to safety.

Throughout the weekend we had collected hundreds of rounds of machine-gun ammunition and by the final day they made a considerable pile. The safest way to dispose of them was a controlled

explosion. The RAF team went into action and, at a site 200 metres (600 feet) away, set off a very impressive explosion. The detonator was pressed by Professor Aston on the occasion of his birthday.

We laid out all our finds on the ground and, with the help of Bob Spangler and Bernie Ford, the air-crash investigator, located each piece in the approximate position it would have occupied in the aircraft.

Conclusion

It is probably appropriate to end with two pieces of information. The first is that the men who died never had a memorial and that large pieces of the B–17 and one of the two machine guns will be used to create one. The second is Bernie Ford's crash report reprinted on page 181 the dry analytical facts behind which we all felt the presence of the young aircrew who gave their lives in the Second World War.

Opposite: The bomb-disposal crew from RAF Wittering – with just a fraction of the machine-gun rounds found on the site.

Below: Hosing down the Browning machine gun. A live round was later found in the breach.

B–17 Site, Reedham Marsh, June/July 1998

The Air-Crash Investigator Report – Bernie Ford

'The probable sequence of events was as follows. Three B–17s entered cloud on their descent. At some time the No. 2 (Pease) left the formation. This may have been due to an engine failure because one propeller was found in the feathered 1 position, i.e. the condition that the pilot would select following an engine failure. The distraction caused by this emergency may have led the pilot to become disorientated. The aircraft was seen by the other members of the formation to come out of cloud in a steep dive at high speed. It passed below the other two aircraft and then executed a vigorous pull-out, which led it to fly in front of the leader. In the subsequent collision, at about 800 feet, the entire tail unit (aft of the waist gunmen) was severed. The aircraft continued to climb for a short period before falling back into the lead aircraft. This collision caused the lead aircraft to break in two. Evidence for this is from eyewitnesses in the No. 3 aircraft and also damage to the second propeller from the No. 2 aircraft indicating that it had hit something round and very solid, possibly a gun. The No. 2 aircraft then fell at an angle close to the vertical and crashed into a drainage ditch at an estimated speed of about 200 mph. This estimate of speed is from extensive experience of the state of the wreckage where the impact speed was known.'

Previous page: Professor Aston's birthday present goes up in smoke – a satisfactory conclusion to the dig.

Opposite: Sue Francis takes digital still of the crash wreckage – cameraman Dennis Borrow and soundman Doug Dredger capture the moment.

Following page: The end of the 'Bombers' shoot. Relief and elation were mixed in equal measure. Simon Raikes, Brendan Hughes and myself couldn't resist getting our hands on the machine guns. The cameo piece of nose artwork in the background made a perfect backdrop.

Above: The final film is on-lined. Graham Dixon, in the sepulchral gloom of an edit suite, puts in the finishing touches.

Graham: There are loads of shots of Stewart I could include.

Tim: The other thing that you must define is the reason we see a dog dashing around every so often on the site!

Graham: The dog is a pet belonging to one of the diggers. He travels everywhere with her.

Our key feeling was that the programme worked and achieved a good balance between the reality of the archaeology, the enjoyment of the cameo and the content of the trenches. From the start Graham had intended to use the golf as a humorous counterpoint to the archaeology and this worked well. Phil did an excellent job as our eye into the cameo and the final sequences in which the metal was produced were great. We

Behind the Scenes at *Time Team*

needed more of a sensation of struggling in the early scenes and some clearing up of trench numbers – but in general we both felt that the programme worked and did the classic *Time Team* job of realistically facing up to a difficult site and making the process enjoyable.

There were some hard decisions along the way – bits of film we had to leave out. This is inevitable. Some of Victor Ambrus's drawings, for example, were excellent but featured material that we had not found and therefore seemed out of place. We had not addressed the way the site had been handled previously or the issue of local helpers using divining rods. There is a point when you have to go with the director's vision, which creates a programme that has its own reality. This is the nature of a combined creative process.

Epilogue

When I think back over the programmes featured in this book each one evokes strong memories and images of what we achieved. The cavers and diggers at Cooper's Hole covered in mud and hauling up their improvised sled full of material from deep inside the cave. The mass of pottery falling from the digger bucket in Burslem and the hundreds of friendly faces that watched it happen. The weight of the machine guns from the trenches on the 'Bombers' shoot. The sparks flying from ships' nails as they were hammered by the smith at Smallhythe. The trenches deep in the woods at Beauport Park and the final glint of sunlight on the piece of iron. Chris captured some of these moments and preserved them in his photographs.

Above: Brendan Hughes taking a well-earned rest from the rigours of second unit directing.

It is difficult to say which was my favourite programme. Although we did not find a lot at Beauport Park the dig was a great example of the *Time Team* working through a hypothesis. It showed that an honest process can be interesting and that there is no need to find a body or gold dish to make archaeology interesting. I hope

Behind the Scenes at *Time Team*

what comes across is that after forty programmes and seven years of working together all of us still enjoy the series and are thrilled when we somehow manage to pluck triumph from disaster.

It is worth emphasizing that each *Time Team* shoot is a unique piece of archaeology that will be an important addition to the archaeological record. It could provide the key to a particular puzzle that has existed for years. It is probably true to say that few of the excavations would have taken place if they hadn't been chosen and funded by a *Time Team* programme. In this sense we all feel proud of the fact that *Time Team* has made a considerable contribution to the historical record by investing in these sites, and that our work will be an invaluable source for the future.

Time Team is not just about the archaeology. Each programme is also a human drama about overcoming practical problems and keeping to a story-line that will ultimately carry viewers with it. It is a drama that often takes place away from the cameras, and I hope that when you see the photographs in this book and read how the programmes evolved you will feel that you have had a chance to eavesdrop on what goes on behind the scenes, and have an increased understanding of the archaeological techniques we use. I hope, too, that you will share in the excitement and elation the *Time Team* group still feels when, usually at the last moment, the evidence unfolds.

Above: *It's been a long year and sometimes we all need a bit of a lie down! Mr Robinson is probably dreaming of where he'll be heading next on* Time Team.

Index

Page numbers in *italics* refer to captions

Acknowledgments

Tim Taylor and Chris Bennett would like to thank all of *Time Team* and its crew for the cooperation that made this book possible.

Particular thanks go to the following people, who checked specific details in the text:

Chapter 1: Andy Currant, Bob Smart and Bob Croft.

Chapter 2: Bill Klemperer and Noel Boothroyd.

Chapter 3: Guy de la Bédoyère.

Chapter 4: Gustav Milne and Ian Friel.

Chapter 5: Ian McLachlan.

With special thanks to Liz Warner, Time Team's current Commissioning Editor, for her support during these programmes.

Finally, with thanks to Karla Goodman for relentlessly pursuing all the contributors and collating additional information.